# THE NEW BOTTOM LINE

# THE NEW BOTTOM LINE

## PEOPLE AND LOYALTY IN BUSINESS

---

William B. Walton, Sr.
Cofounder, Holiday Inns, Inc.
with
Dr. Mel Lorentzen

*1817*

Harper & Row, Publishers, San Francisco

Cambridge, Hagerstown, New York, Philadelphia, Washington
London, Mexico City, São Paulo, Singapore, Sydney

FIRST EDITION

**Library of Congress Cataloging-in-Publication Data**

Walton, William B.
  The new bottom line.

  1. Employee motivation.  2. Employees, Training of.
3. Leadership.  I. Lorentzen, Mel.  II. Title.
HF5549.5.M63W35 1986      658.3      85–45369
ISBN 0–06–250910–1

86  87  88  89  90  HC  10  9  8  7  6  5  4  3  2  1

*For Geneva*
*beloved wife and praying partner*
*through it all.*

*And for my Holiday Inns Family,*
*who put service above self*
*to make the miracle happen.*

# Contents

# Introduction
## *The Company Attitude:* Thinking Right About People

The man who was an officer of Xerox asked me his question with apparent amazement over the latest story he'd read about Holiday Inns, Inc., in the *Wall Street Journal.*

"How do you get away with it, Bill?"

He wasn't the first executive to be mystified by certain company policies that I took for granted as chief operating officer.

I couldn't give him an analytical answer. I knew, of course, that we were a maverick outfit that caused people in the lodging industry to shake their heads over things we did that struck them as bizarre. An unstoppable entrepreneur like Kemmons Wilson, who started the whole glorious affair, was prone to throw away the book and trust his instincts.

And it worked. For us, anyway. At the time.

But, is that all there was to it? Beginner's luck, maybe? Inspired genius? Good timing? I suppose a little of each must have played a part in the Holiday Inns saga. But even if you add the necessary common sense, guts, and tenacity, you still haven't got the whole explanation.

Reflecting on it after three decades with the company, I'm more convinced than ever that the secret of our sixteen-year rise from nothing to the top of the hotel industry was simply this: we had the right Attitude about people.

That may sound like nonsense to business administration sophisticates. In my opinion, though, that right Attitude is the very essence of excellence.

It holds the secret of survival.

It drove the overextended personal computer manufacturers, for example, to spend a thousand and one sleepless nights in the past several years trying to break through with "user friendly" equipment.

After years of depersonalized and dehumanized theories and practices, American big business is confronting the stark fact that it has lost its credibility with the people. It forgot to listen and failed to respond.

At the same time, and maybe for that very reason, another phenomenon increasingly dominates the present business age. It comes as a considerable surprise to many executive suite occupants that personal entrepreneurship has come galloping out of the past and started doing its tricks again in the center ring! Undignified, maybe, but it's what the crowd stands up and cheers about.

In April 1984, *Inc.* magazine published a special fifth-anniversary issue with a cover proclaiming in bold red and black type: "America is once again becoming a nation of risk takers, and the way we do business will never be the same. . . ."

The cover feature story heralded "The Age of the Entrepreneur." Among so-called "Prophets of the New Age" it pictured were Fred Smith, Federal Express; F. Kenneth Iverson, Nucor; Steven Jobs, Apple Computer; Bill Nourse, Brookmeade Hardware; and Thomas Carter, Carter Electronics.

In a lengthy interview with the magazine, Allan A. Kennedy, coauthor of *Corporate Cultures* (with Terrence E. Deal) identified at least three factors that contribute to this trend: the rise of a financially more secure middle class, the economy's shift into the service sector, and the inherent entrepreneurial spirit that has traditionally characterized the American people.

In the current scramble for recovery of respectability, business is exhibiting a fixation for excellence—however it can be defined. Executives are scrutinizing the record of classic business successes to find out, if they can, what determined the difference between making it and making it *big*.

Thomas J. Peters and Robert H. Waterman Jr. did us all a good turn by titling their bestseller *In Search of Excellence*. Their documentation of selected American companies that have stayed on top suggests that excellence has to be sought. It doesn't just materialize automatically. And it has to be genuine. There's plenty of fool's gold along the trail to mislead the searcher.

Excellence isn't brilliance. Or bravado. Or getting the breaks. It's not even some super capacity to make things work well. At any level, but especially at the executive, it's ultimately respect for human dignity—without pretense, without hypocrisy.

In the centuries-old tradition of Jews and Christians alike, excellence is loving your neighbor, the commandment second in rank only to loving God. It's responsiveness to human needs.

The Attitude.

When I wrote the constitution for the fledgling Holiday Inns system back in 1956, I stated "that we intend to build a corporation and a business based on the recognition of the dignity of all people and on Christian principles, especially man's love for his fellow man."

We meant it. We worked hard at it. A decade and a half later, we had become the largest hotel company in the world, with annual revenues approaching two billion dollars.

But it isn't always the noblest motivation that launches a great enterprise. Holiday Inns started with a mad dad.

Kemmons Wilson came home to Memphis furious at the lodging industry after a 1951 trip to Washington, D.C., with his wife Dorothy and their five children. His experience on the road, having to stay in fleabag tourist camps in the country or in fancy hotels in cities, triggered a passion to create an alternative.

Because he was a builder and developer, he wasted no time in putting up his first prototypes—not one but four—right in his hometown. The architectural style was a sort of glorified postwar ranch house. The room rate was $6 double per night! He named them from the popular 1942 Bing Crosby movie, *Holiday Inn*.

Right from the start, their volume of business proved his point: the American traveling public was overdue for clean, comfortable accommodations at a reasonable price.

Kemmons didn't know the meaning of market research, and he didn't have to. He knew instinctively that there must be millions of Americans as disgruntled as he was about overnight lodgings that were either squalid or snooty, with nothing in between. Because he himself was a victim of the situation, he knew what he wanted to change. Everything!

For starters, he didn't think it was fair to charge families extra for each of their children, so he instituted the "Children Free" policy.

He knew families didn't like to leave their pets at home when they went on a trip, so he provided free kennels and pet food at his motels.

He was tired of extra charges and the whole tipping system, so he offered free ice, free baby beds, free TV in every room, free advance reservations, and self-service luggage handling.

He understood firsthand some of the special concerns of traveling families, so he provided baby-sitter references, physicians and dentists on call, restaurant service at reasonable prices, and swimming pools and playground equipment.

And he ordered 6'8" mattresses so tall people wouldn't have to sleep with their feet hanging over the edge of the bed!

Everybody is so used to those things now that they forget how innovative, even revolutionary, such provisions were in the years just after the close of World War II. People traveling through Memphis could hardly believe their eyes and ears when they stopped at an economical Holiday Inn with all of its free benefits.

Entrepreneur that he was, Kemmons dreamed of bigger things—a chain of 400 inns, maybe 500, lining Route 66 right across the country! He persuaded his good friend and construction business cohort, Wallace E. Johnson, to join him as partner, and the two of them together with Elmer "Jack" Ladd and E. B. "Barney" McCool, started trying to sell franchises to fellow board members of the National Home Builders Association.

Probably the main reason for the instant success of Kemmons's first Memphis motels was that he was in fact the customer. Everything he worked into the plan was to satisfy a need of his own. He was not thinking like a promoter but like a user. "This is what I want when I stop someplace along the highway. This is what my family would enjoy in an overnight stay."

The informing genius of the original concept was: "Give the people what they want."

The people. Yes.

Holiday Inns was definitely a people story from the Wilsons on—possibly the greatest of its kind in American business annals. It was management's concern for our people, and those people's concern for our guests, that earned us accolades and awards in the years that followed.

To start with, though, fewer than ten of the home builders responded to Kemmons and Wallace. And soon there was real trouble, threatening possible court action, because there was no corporation adequately organized to back up the franchise promises.

So in 1955, Kemmons and Wallace invited me to join them to put the idea together organizationally and to run the day-to-day operations. There was no franchise model for me to copy, and although I wasn't a complete ignoramus by any means, I didn't know a thing about the hotel business. I was a happily married family man who had built up a thriving Memphis law practice over the previous ten years. It surely wasn't the business proposition that captivated me—not at the $500-a-month salary they promised.

It must have been the idea! Back in the years after the Revolutionary War, my ancestral namesake, Captain William Walton, had operated an inn on the toll road he owned between what are now Knoxville and Nashville. Nostalgia and sentiment drew pictures in my mind of those early Americans hitching their horses outside and then relaxing around a warm fireside in the snug little inn, enjoying good food and tall tales and laughter.

Lawyer or not, I was and am an incurable romantic. Anyway, I said yes to the deal with Kemmons and Wallace over a glass of orange soda at a home builders' picnic.

We each brought to the relationship our individual strengths and skills. Kemmons was the dreamer, Wallace the financier. The *New York Times* would later call us a "troika," and it said of me: "His forte is administration, his touch humane."

So started what would be the most harrowing and yet rewarding adventure of my life for the next twenty years and more. I had enough business sense to know that in no time at all others would be copying Holiday Inn basics like a swimming pool and big beds and coffee shops. I had to find an added dimension to keep us distinctive. And find it fast.

That's when the Attitude seed was sown.

Between the eighteenth-century Walton and the twentieth-century Wilson, I saw a shining prospect of fostering goodwill among travelers by giving them a richly pleasurable fireside human relationship. In all my subsequent years with Holiday Inns, Inc.—thirty of them until I retired in 1985—I never substituted any other vision for that one, even when things got very complicated and controversial.

It was that Attitude toward people—our own in the company, and the wonderful public we were here to serve— that guided my earliest formulations of the Holiday Inns charter and constitution, the organization of the franchise system, the compilation of the operating manual, and every administrative order I issued as executive vice-president and then as president.

My argument with Holiday Inns management in later years was over the issue of whether the people were truly well served by the policy changes being urged and adopted.

It was my opinion then, and is my settled conviction today, that a fundamental shift in corporate focus at the top management level led Holiday Inns down a path that effectively obliterated its distinctiveness in the whole travel and tourism industry and made it just one of the pack.

But, for all that, its phenomenal rise in the first fifteen to twenty years to the top of the lodging industry worldwide happened while the focus was fixed intensely on a people Attitude of respect and neighborly love. I am everlastingly grateful to God that I was around then to see what could happen when a big business put a higher priority on a better life for the men, women, and children who were its clients than on the corporation's fiscal bottom line.

I want to take you behind the Holiday Inns success scene to illustrate how the quest for that will-o'-the-wisp called excellence adds supreme zest to the executive role, while delivering superior satisfaction. It's the highest kind of adventure because it explores human frontiers.

But excellence isn't always easy to spot, since titles and job descriptions can hide the facts. You have to be able to distinguish between in-charge people who simply flip switches, and in-control people who actually generate power.

Promotions in the pecking order don't guarantee excellence. Going higher doesn't mean getting better, as the Peter principle makes clear. People get moved up on the corporate scale because of meritorious performance, only to find themselves at a new level whose demands exceed their abilities. Their output deteriorates into relative mediocrity, and they get locked into frustration or failure. Excellence at the management level calls for something besides mere coping and controlling.

The key is *Attitude*. A former president of Northwestern University, Walter Dill Scott, pointed out that a person's mental attitude plays a far more important part in success or failure than does mental capacity.

Even before it is performance, then, excellence is point of view. From my earliest days as an officer at Holiday Inns, I stressed the company Attitude above everything else.

Why? Because a good attitude is the best motivation.

And motivation in a business has to start at the top. Managers are the prime motivators in any organization. They are the ones who move people to peak achievement. John D. Rockefeller is credited with saying, "The ability to deal with people is as purchasable a commodity as sugar or coffee. And I pay more for that ability than for any other under the sun."

Management attitude will mean more than anything else in replacing mediocrity with excellence. But one can never assume that people at the upper levels have the right attitude. In fact, the early retirement roster of corporate leaders from Manhattan to Malibu shows how frequently they lack it.

What do those people in power clutch most tightly? Security. They don't want to lose the authority they've acquired. They guard and defend their prerogatives because they don't want anyone else to appear to be able to do what they can do. They do not want to retire or to go to work under someone else, because they relish their image of being in charge.

Such executives know they don't have job security under the prevailing system. They dread the next step, aware that it will require them to step down or to step out. What alternate security measures do they devise?

1. Some try to get the rules changed, to make an exception for their particular case.
2. Some try to create new titles or new status to perpetuate their official standing until they die.
3. Some groom their heirs and protégés who, when they assume control of operations, will continue to take orders from the senior mentor.
4. Some make deals with the competition to share all the company secrets by becoming highly paid consultants to others.
5. Some line up new business ventures where they can maintain at least figurehead leadership rank.
6. Some amass personal fortunes so they can buy continuing influence through board memberships.
7. Some turn to philanthropic activity, through which they can exert financial clout to make things happen according to their own plans.
8. Some of the men divorce faithful wives and marry frisky young women to prolong their delusions of unabated attractiveness and virility.
9. Some create paper kingdoms where they rule over fictitious subjects.
10. Some turn to religion and try to foster a new image of personal piety that will cover a multitude of sins and rationally justify their making a substitution of better things for the old ways.

Ironically, the security sought in all of the above ways remains just as elusive as ever, and the anticipated satisfactions are disappointingly scant. Life has not become empty of things to do, surely, but they all seem fairly flat and futile.

With chilling realism, the writer of Ecclesiastes sums up this situation:

I saw that under the sun the race is not to the swift, nor the battle to the strong, nor bread to the wise, nor riches to the intelligent, nor favor to men of skill; but time and chance happen to them all . . . I have seen slaves on horses, and princes walking on foot like slaves . . . All is vanity and a striving after wind.

Obviously, something more basic than political savvy or professional clout is necessary to secure a top job in management.

This drive to achieve status is a concern not only for those at the summit of business power, but for those on the way up. They especially have an appetite for personal success secrets and miracle methods of management. Advancement is their immediate preoccupation, and they face constant threats from peer competition. Many of them favor graduate business school training, while they take a dim view of seat-of-the-pants entrepreneurs. It comes as quite a shock to such young wizards to find out that country people built commercial empires without the benefit of the almighty M.B.A.!

I want to tell the would-be survivors and the would-be arrivers what I believe about attitude. It's the explanation of why Holiday Inns made it big on the twentieth-century American business scene.

There are two main reasons why it's important for me to explain that.

First, I discovered the hard way how a bad attitude can destroy what matters most in life. You shouldn't have to make the same mistakes I did. The great philosopher Santayana said, Those who cannot remember the past are condemned to repeat it.

Second, I am absolutely persuaded that you, whatever your sphere or level of responsibility might be, can be a forceful motivator of others by personally developing what I call the Attitude of Excellence.

Remember, attitude is the way you think about people and act toward them—daily. Whether you are chair of the board or chair of the clean-up committee, your attitude will make the difference between executive excellence or mediocre management. It will determine whether you motivate people or only manipulate them.

In the first sixteen years of my administering day-to-day affairs at Holiday Inns, I saw our attitude transform a chain of four motels in Memphis into an international system of nearly 2,000 hotels employing 150,000 enthusiastic and loyal men and women and entertaining a quarter of a million satisfied guests every night.

It wasn't those statistics that mattered primarily, even though they impressed Wall Street a lot. It was what they symbolized about the spirit in the organization. We meant it when we said we were people-centered.

I used to tell our innkeepers at their training sessions that anybody could build a bunch of $12' \times 27'$ rooms and rent them out for a night. That's not what defined a Holiday Inn. Rather, it was the attitude of our employees toward each other and toward our guests.

Why do I contend that modern business management needs the added dimension of attitude if it is to achieve a peak of excellence? For one thing, the whole library of recent literature about management deals almost entirely with ways and means instead of with the dynamics underlying it all.

The biggest fallacy in the field, though, is applying the term *management* to the control of people. Management thus understood is nothing more than manipulation, the very opposite of motivation.

Management means having to keep your eye on people all the time to see that they are functioning according to orders.

Motivation, by contrast, means being able to turn your back with confidence that the people's attitude, or inner drive, will carry them through their assignments.

In other words, you manage a business, but you motivate human beings.

So let's get rid of this ambiguity about management. Even the highly touted MBWA (Management By Wandering Around) has to be understood as a principle of letting people know that you are interested in the work they are doing and want to recognize its significance. If you wander around simply to keep an eye on things, then you're duplicating the intrusive and oppressive role of Big Brother.

My whole point is that a good employer/employee relationship, like every other, must be built on trust. Without it, managers are little different from wardens or guards who see to it that everyone takes orders and moves in lockstep. Guards never turn their backs because they do not trust anybody. Their authority is the gun.

Let's face it. Plenty of companies do operate a lot like prisons. People working there feel as if they are under a life sentence with no hope of parole, simply because they have to make a living. The easiest way to survive is to start when the bell rings, stop when it rings again, and avoid any independent thinking in between.

It works, some will argue. Sure, the way prisons always work. They demean the human personality and destroy almost all chance for a constructive role in society. One of the gross misnomers for our prisons is "correctional system." As presently constituted and administered, they actually aggravate the national crime problem. At the heart of the prison crisis is the fact that they are "management" in the extreme, without any motivational attitude.

Another major fallacy about management is that it can be successful if you use the right techniques or gimmicks. For instance, take the fad of one minute management—one minute for praise and one minute for criticism—as the way to get people to produce. I readily agree that you can do a lot to motivate people with an appropriate word or two at the opportune time. But to suggest that such occasional blips across the screen of personnel relations will add up to a full-color picture of contentment and profitability is wishful thinking.

A lot is said about incentives in management theory. Well, a mechanical rabbit on a stick provides incentive for a good dog race. In business, as many people cynically comment, the whole thing readily degenerates into a rat race, however, where the goal is to devour or be devoured. That kind of incentive—the survival of the fittest concept—may be a powerful motivation to animal instinct, but it has no regard for human dignity nor for the mightiest power in the world—love.

Many years ago, the witty British journalist Malcolm Muggeridge reviewed in *Esquire* a book about Charles Darwin and his Galapagos Islands explorations, which contributed so much to his evolutionary hypothesis. Commenting on "survival of the fittest," Muggeridge observed that it might seem to make good sense until you come up against the "fittest" person in all human history who was not guilty of any weakness or wrongdoing, according to the verdict of his trial judge. Yet he was executed on a cross. Not only was this an exception to Darwin's theory, as Muggeridge viewed it, but also the inverse power of that sacrifice of love radically altered history from then until now.

I'm no theologian. I'm a businessman. While I cannot explain the meaning and impact of the death of Jesus, I can see this: if God cared enough for humanity to make that kind of intervention to save us from self-destruction, then undoubtedly something about us is eminently worth saving. Insofar as my life as an executive affects other lives, then, I'm to care about whatever it is in them that God sees as so valuable.

And that worth, in my opinion, cannot be mere animal instinct for survival. Rather, it must be the divine drive planted within us to reach the highest peak of our human potential—in God's purpose and by his help. After all, creatures made in God's image had to be intended for something glorious. In my vocabulary, a rat race doesn't fit that description.

In the business world, then, I feel that it is the mandate and mission of an excellent manager to create conditions in the workplace where people will be energized and encouraged to stretch toward the greatest self-realization. With that fundamental motivation, everything that follows is bound to be good for the business enterprise as well.

That Attitude, therefore, makes practical sense.

And that Attitude, I repeat, must begin with the top person. In our business, if an innkeeper shuffled in after ten in the morning, sloppily dressed, and lounged against the front desk holding a drip-stained mug of coffee, that innkeeper was modeling whatever he or she expected from everybody else who worked there.

Such an attitude is neither self-respecting nor considerate of others. It says, "I see myself as a slob." It says, "I see the rest of you as undeserving of my best." It's an attitude of contempt that is bound to undermine morale and hurt business.

By contrast, the Attitude we built into the charter of Holiday Inns was truly a company Attitude. By that, I don't mean simply that it was the official posture of the corporation. Above all, it emphasized that we saw ourselves—all of us, from chair of the board to cleaning people—as a company of people. We were comrades in a crusade to bring to the American traveling public a highway haven, a home away from home, to rest and refresh them.

In the military we talk about a ship's company. In the entertainment world, we talk about a theater company. The word *company* is an English form of the French for "companion." It carries the idea of fellowship, literally of sharing your bread.

Managers who forget that they are members of a human "company" risk making all kinds of unnecessary mistakes in relating to people. To have a company Attitude in the business realm, those in management must respect their associates in several ways that I'm going to illustrate for you out of my own experiences.

Anyone who has the faith and fortitude to persist at developing this Attitude can build a work environment where employees can enjoy a satisfying sense of self-worth through a job well done.

Many have tried to define that Attitude succinctly. One of my favorite renditions came to my desk many years ago in the form of a reprint from *Parade* magazine. It reads like this:

For the New Year:
A Short Course in Human Relations
The SIX most important words:
"I admit I made a mistake"

The FIVE most important words:
"You did a good job"
The FOUR most important words:
"What is your opinion?"
The THREE most important words:
"If you please"
The TWO most important words:
"Thank you"
The ONE most important word:
"We"
The LEAST important word:
"I"

People in management ought to commit this to memory!

Executives and entrepreneurs may not mix any better than oil and water, as documented in a 1985 Gallup Poll conducted for the *Wall Street Journal*. But if they both want to be the best at what they're doing, they need to take a page or two out of each other's books. As an executive who was teamed for more than twenty years with one of this century's most colorful entrepreneurs, I learned that Attitude did more than anything else to make contrasting personalities work well together. I hope it helps you in your situation.

After more than half a century as a working man, beginning in the Great Depression when I was twelve and my father left home, I'm sure of this: it's the easiest thing in the world to get away with mediocrity.

But to achieve excellence in a society that settles for less takes some real doing. Getting your attitude straight is the start. On that bedrock foundation, you can build for the future—your own as well as the company's. If you believe in people and treat them right, the people will follow and honor you. Only then can you make any valid claim to be a leader.

Excellence is not picked up in business seminars. It is a product of personal integrity. Yours.

Excellence does not come by chance.

It comes by choice.

Yours.

# I. THINKING RIGHT ABOUT MOTIVATING PEOPLE

# 1. Building Morale
## Do the People Feel Happy?

At Holiday Inns headquarters every Christmas Eve day, I made it a point to spend the entire morning going from department to department, wishing every individual a Merry Christmas and thanking them for their service and loyalty to the company.

The only one who ever made part of the rounds with me was Kemmons Wilson's mother, Ruby, affectionately called Doll, who related in a special way to the women in the drapery department, since she'd done the famous chartreuse-and-yellow interior decorating of the first fifty Holiday Inns.

One Christmas Eve, Mrs. Wilson and I headed across the parking lot toward the drapery department building. In a cold sleet, as we trudged through the slushy snow, I said, "Doll, you have no business being out here."

"Sugar," she retorted, "I got no business being any other place. Those ladies are waiting for me right now. I wouldn't disappoint them for anything."

Sure enough, when we got there, several had brought cakes and candies and cookies. They had a table festively set, waiting for Doll. With her characteristic warmth, she hugged and kissed every person in that department. Believe me, they were one happy bunch of women at that moment. She was the mother of the chairman of the board and a leader in the company in her own right, and they loved her!

Lots of people, hearing stories like that, called us sentimental for our informal and people-oriented attitude. But scores of thousands of men and women who worked for Holiday Inns knew they were appreciated by the top leadership. With the high morale pumped up by the Attitude, they rallied to our cause with service to the public that made our name a household word.

Happy, well-trained employees were the moving force behind Holiday Inn's success—no doubt about it.

When the right attitude is in place, 85 to 90% of a company's motivational problems are solved. Attitude and morale are two sides of the same coin.

The worst occupational hazard for top management is losing touch with people. Whether barricaded in the board room or guarded by a phalanx of administrative assistants, some top managers operate as if the human race existed exclusively in flowcharts and balance sheets.

To them, people are statistics. Employees tend to become ciphers in a corporate formula. The public is hardly anything more than a market research grid.

Such a mentality makes efficiency a synonym for excellence. Ledger ink replaces blood. Executives make pronouncements, as one news reporter observed about one of our officers in later years, that are "cash register remarks." Human beings are treated as disposable components in the corporate machine, easily discarded as soon as they break down.

Such contempt for people infiltrated our ranks, too, even at the very start. One of our original department heads cynically commented to me one day, "You have to assume every employee is stealing from you, and then fix it so he can't." Not surprisingly, that man's department was a disaster area, and his career with us was one of the shorter on record.

Business research today shows that high technology, with its magical possibilities, ironically aggravates the problem of disregarding the individual. John Naisbitt identifies one current trend that struggles to compensate for high technology with what he calls "high touch." The more advanced our machines become, he concludes, the more humane our treatment of people must be. How could we ever have forgotten this?

As I traveled the Holiday Inn system in the Learjet, I could be in Memphis, Minneapolis, and Miami all in the same day. In each city, I'd visit as many inns as possible. There, even if it was twenty-six stories, I'd cover as much territory as I had time for, starting at the top and using the stairwell to make my way from floor to floor. In the hallways, I'd pause to greet people who were cleaning rooms, calling each by name, which I could read on their badges.

Sometimes I'd take an extra few minutes with housekeepers to underscore the importance of what they and their staff were doing to help the company.

I have no patience with managers who say, "I don't have time to visit with the employees. I don't have time to go into various departments and discuss their work."

To such self-important executives, my comment is this: "The first thing you lack, then, is skill in managing your time intelligently."

The people are the company. How can they be overlooked or slighted?

In 1956, as I wrestled to compose one of my first speeches for the people at Holiday Inns, I kept searching for a word I could use instead of *employees*. It wasn't a problem of being misunderstood or resented if I stuck with the conventional term. Everybody would know whom I was talking about, of course.

But we were launching a new Attitude as well as a new approach in the lodging industry. So I named our people "The Holiday Inn Family." Then, with my creative juices at full tide, I substituted the words *guests* for the usual *customers.* The first directive I sent out to the inns was to take down the sign that said "Manager" and replace it with one that said "Innkeeper"!

All of those changes were more than word games, because our fundamental operating philosophy aimed to create roadside lodgings with an atmosphere of fireside human relationship. What we wanted to do for the public, we first had to do inside the company for our own people.

Some critics will probably cluck their tongues and snarl "Paternalism!" That could be true, if employee *control* had been our intention. Rather, though, we wanted to develop working conditions and an esprit de corps where our workers could find happiness and take personal pride in freely contributing to a united effort—an effort that meant, ultimately, to make highway travelers comfortable and contented whenever they stopped at any inn where the star atop our Great Sign had guided them.

The way to be happy yourself, as Judy Garland used to sing, is to "make someone happy."

Ernest R. Breech, who accomplished near miracles in pulling Bendix, Ford, and TWA out of the doldrums years ago, was asked how he attracted and kept people who were both practical and visionary. He stressed the primary importance of a happy working atmosphere and a team spirit pervading the ranks, all the way from top managers to mechanics and flight crews. Their personal interest in doing a good job depended on their feeling they were a part of the company. He knew that it took more than a paycheck to generate a sense of worth in their work.

At Holiday Inns, Attitude was all. Spreading from the top, it caught the imagination of the entire work force, directly influencing all contacts with the public in every inn.

And it was always a case of "As goes the innkeeper, so goes the inn." How I stressed this in my address to each group that went through our training program!

"When a new Holiday Inn is completed, it's only cold brick and mortar until you and your people inhabit it with that warmth and cordiality that make a guest want to keep coming back. You've got to breathe hospitality into the material structure."

They not only had to talk Attitude, they had to demonstrate it, sometimes in near-heroic ways.

On several occasions, inns had to provide emergency shelter for stranded motorists or displaced residents of a community when there was some natural disaster like a blizzard. Even if the crowd in the inn overflowed its capacity by a third or a half, the innkeeper would furnish space in lobbies and meeting rooms as well as available guest rooms, along with blankets, food, and hot drinks. It was the old innkeeping tradition to which we were dedicated, putting the comfort and safety of the public above the temporary inconvenience to the staff and above any thought of profit to the establishment.

If management doesn't have the right attitude toward its own people, though, it will write job descriptions or issue directives to employees that have no built-in motivational power.

At Holiday Inns, we could admonish our desk clerks, "Be courteous," and hang it on the wall as a motto. But the result might be nothing more than a pasted-on smile and a mechanical "May I help you?" Bare admonishment is counterproductive to good morale because it imposes just one more obligation. It has simply added another company rule.

By contrast, to make courtesy the company spirit and to generate employee happiness, the assignment has to be both meaningful and manageable.

In the hospitality business, the meaning behind courtesy to guests as they approach the front desk at an inn is fairly obvious. Most of them arrive physically weary from a long day's journey, emotionally strained by travel problems or bickering children or anxieties about what they've left behind them and what they face tomorrow.

Whether in so many words or not, the cheerful greeting at the front desk should communicate to them, "Relax, friends. You're going to be well taken care of here." That promising reassurance can do a whole lot to change an anxious traveler into a grateful guest, we found out. Employee happiness has a direct bearing on customer satisfaction, and it boosts business results.

Every business, whether it manufactures a product or provides a service, can apply the principle of people centeredness. What we especially tried to do was to impress on our workers what their *role* was, not only their duties.

At an inn's front desk, for example, the attendant does not simply run through the clerical routine of securing basic check-in information and handing out room keys. He or she is the company greeter, the welcomer, the management's host who extends house privileges to an honored guest.

Any employee, in any business, who has direct contact with the public should embody cordiality and good humor. To do so, of course, they must be happy on the job.

But the daily routine of business produces plenty of disturbances to one's humor and happiness. You have to work at being courteous. It's easy when you're fresh and things are going well. But it takes courage and control when you are tired and your customer is hard to get along with.

For instance, what does our representative inn clerk do when the role as a welcomer is frustrated by the fact that every room is taken on a given night, and a bedraggled family of four stands in front of the desk desperate for a place to stay? My son Rusty worked the front desk at inns for a while, and he tells me this is a horrible moment of truth for the clerk!

That family stopped at the Holiday Inn because they didn't see a "No Vacancy" sign outside. That was not an oversight by the management. Our operating manual absolutely forbid the posting of such a sign under any circumstances.

Misleading the public? Cruel and inhuman treatment? Hardly. Do you know what it's like to drive down a lonely stretch of highway late at night and see nothing but "No Vacancy" blinking its neon at you from every longed-for haven? Nobody wants you to stop and bother them. The sign really says to the traveler, "Go away." It's Joseph and Mary in Bethlehem all over again. It's depressing.

Our point in eliminating that sign from Holiday Inn equipment had the public's best interest at heart. In actual fact, an innkeeper might have a room available if there had been a last-minute cancellation or a no-show without a guarantee.

But suppose the innkeeper really does have full occupancy. If the business is to rent rooms and every room is taken, in effect he or she is out of business.

I never saw room renting as the primary business of Holiday Inns. Our business was the hospitality business. We could surely extend hospitality to discouraged travelers, vacancies or not. Our clerks were instructed always to do what they could, first of all, to help the disappointed prospects relax. At least offer a seat in the lobby and a cup of coffee or a cold drink. Our challenge was to raise their sagging spirits.

Second, contact was to be made with a Holiday Inn in the vicinity or another motel of like quality in the area to locate an optional room to recommend to the traveler. Incidentally, we also could offer the services of our reservations system to make sure they had accommodations secured for the next night of their journey!

If all efforts failed to turn up lodgings, the clerk could give a reasonable explanation of why the territory was so fully booked, invite them to use the public washrooms and the vending machines, and send them on their way into the night somewhat refreshed and heartened by the sympathetic attempts to help.

There's a vast difference between renting and hosting. We felt we were never out of the business of being nice to people who needed help along the road. Later on, when they were in a more fortunate situation to choose where they would stop for a night, you can bet they didn't forget Holiday Inns!

Helpfulness to others brings its own reward. When employees discover the meaning of their job is to see how useful they can be to someone in need, they are much more likely to be happy at work than if they perfunctorily go through the minimal motions.

It's my firm belief that God has put into the hearts of every one of us a desire to love and to be loved, to achieve and to be accepted by others, to be important to somebody, to help. This is especially strong in young people before they get infected with the virus of cynicism and doubt. They might not improve their attitude just by making more money, but they will have a better outlook if they genuinely feel they are helping others.

When you interpret an employee's role, be sure to include as many suggestions as you can to help the person fill it. Always credit them with wanting to do the most they can, not the least, unless you find evidence to the contrary. In fact, run through a variety of hypothetical situations to see how imaginatively they can cope. The level of morale will rise in anticipation of such chances to show their stuff, rather than drop in fear of unforeseen emergencies.

Every man and woman alive is gifted by God in some special way. It's imperative, therefore, that they believe in themselves, have a good feeling about themselves.

People who have a self-image of worth are going to see value in what they do. This is the Attitude that motivates them to be and to do their best. It's a drive that comes from within people. It's infinitely more powerful than any compulsion imposed from the outside. It gives life the highest meaning—that of mattering!

Making a job responsibility *meaningful* in such ways, however, is only half of the happiness equation. What about making it *manageable* for the employee?

The first duty of supervisors, obviously, is to make sure the employee's basic tasks are sufficiently controllable to allow him or her to meet any other expectations. A worker cannot be happy when assignments are unreasonably heavy or even impossible.

Unrealistic expectations can demoralize a work force faster than anything else I know. Cute slogans like "The impossible takes longer" may lend a spurt of incentive up front, but they aren't nearly enough to carry someone through a tough grind to satisfying results.

Job performance is influenced by many factors. Usually

we think first of worker abilities. Do they have what it takes to do the job? Do they have the intelligence, the skills, the determination, to see it through?

All of that is crucial, naturally. Ability to repair a car doesn't imply ability to repair a watch. A good hairdresser won't necessarily make a good window dresser. Assignments have to be matched with aptitudes. Supervisors at every level deal with this challenge all the time.

Beyond all of that, though, a certain executive attitude makes a high impact on the natural gifts or acquired abilities of workers. In fact, it can make the difference between their success or failure.

Do you have *confidence* in them?

Confidence must be fed from the top. Do you believe the people who work for you can do what you assign them? Do you communicate to them your complete trust in their capabilities? They generally will not have greater confidence in themselves than you show.

Sometimes, on the other hand, the job itself is unrealistic, totally apart from worker ability to do it. I'm not talking about hard work, in fact, just the opposite. Busywork is manageable enough, but it lacks the virtue of mattering.

I have seen too many short-sighted managers make up busywork for their employees. Why?

In some cases, they may do it simply to show who's boss. Or they panic whenever there's the slightest lull in a production schedule and dream up anything just to keep things rolling. Or—and this may be the most disheartening attitude of all—administrators sometimes will commit themselves to a fruitless course of action and pursue it with a passion just to save face for themselves or somebody else. No self-respecting worker finds satisfaction in laboring over projects that don't matter.

As with other businesses, a lot of essential record keeping is involved with desk duty at an inn, which as mere routine might seem to be just so much busywork. In fact, however, all that detail is important, and the clerk cannot afford to bumble through it. Here's the dilemma: the job description emphasizes the clerk's role as greeter, but how can that be fulfilled if the load of paper work is too time consuming?

That's where the wonders of technology can prove their usefulness by speeding up routine processes and redeeming the validity of the seemingly tedious responsibility. But sometimes even a labor-saving machine can be more confining than freeing.

For our accounting needs in those early days, when we were new at almost everything we were doing, we turned to the big name in the industry for equipment. What they offered us was far too cumbersome and expensive for us at that stage. Worse, its operation was so complex that I protested it would require a desk clerk to have a graduate degree from MIT to work it!

We went to Sweda, an organization that was smaller and more flexible, and told them what we needed and why. They came up with a product that cost ten times less to purchase and that could handle our precise accounting needs simply and swiftly.

One of our first franchisees, baseball hero Mickey Mantle, started complaining to the home office that he wasn't making any money at his Joplin, Missouri, inn. This was most unusual, because business was booming elsewhere throughout the system. Upon investigating, we found that one of Mickey's problems was the highly sophisticated accounting machine he had installed—against our recommendation—that was giving his people all sorts of headaches.

The most expensive is never the best when it can't do the job you need done.

The simpler Sweda machine fully satisfied our two demands. First, a normally competent person could operate the equipment in the course of regular duties. Second, and ultimately important, the desk clerk could give priority to the chief role of being a responsive host to the public.

If you serve a machine instead of the machine serving you, you have cramped your style as a human being and have limited your opportunity to share your individual gifts with others. I was in favor of using the very latest available technology, because we knew it was important to keep good books for inn operations. But we knew equally well that we'd have no books to keep if would-be guests were turned off by a desk clerk's preoccupation with button punching. That's why I insisted that we keep *people* conspicuous at the front desk and put the apparatus in the back room!

Once you've taken care of an employee's self-confidence and have controlled the work load, so that worker and job are realistically suited to each other, you must move on to another concern vital to motivating peak performance.

A person with the necessary skills and aptitudes to handle clerical duties at the front desk probably would function with satisfactory efficiency but with no more heart than a robot if she or he didn't also have high morale. A manager does well to see that the concept of service to the public is ingrained in all the employees. A manager also promises, of course, that job achievement will be recognized and rewarded in appropriate compensation and promotion. These are standard criteria of the marketplace to indicate satisfaction with performance.

There's more to morale building than that, though. Any

manager with the right attitude knows that the motivating of employees requires not only job instruction and the supervisor's confidence and indoctrination with company philosophy; motivation also depends on a manager's gaining insight into what makes a particular individual tick.

Business leaders contend all the time with *mis*placement of personnel. A big part of that problem might be alleviated if more attention were given to fulfilling persons, not just to filling positions.

An excellent executive asks if the applicant is likely to grow on the job and thus become a stronger asset to the company. While it's surely necessary to match up skills and aptitudes with duties, it also pays, in less tangible but long-range ways, perhaps, to rate a worker's development potential in a specific slot. That old-fashioned phrase that a person "shows promise" still belongs in the personnel management vocabulary.

How can you tell if it's present in a person? Psychological testing can be useful, of course, along with business references and records of previous performance. But a skilled interviewer will include questions designed to trigger unguarded responses. What can be learned from the applicant's body language or eye movements or voice inflections? Sometimes nonverbal indicators are more trustworthy than words. Depth and breadth of the hiring interview are as important as its focus.

Over and over again, I have seen talented people blossom when planted in the right job soil, with the eventual fruit of happiness in abundance. I've also seen some tragic cases of blight because a person's chances to grow were inhibited by unfortunate misplacement.

Top managers, whether or not they are directly involved

in the hiring process, need to make sure that company policies allow for a reasonable amount of individuality to flourish within the bounds of sensible operations.

Take the man who spends a lot of the time at his desk just staring out the window. Granted, it's possible that he's letting his mind wander from his work. He could be daydreaming about sinking a hole-in-one at the country club or tryng to figure out how to meet his car payments or pondering his doctor's report on the latest physical checkup.

But just maybe he's dreaming up a new sales strategy or an improved production process or even that mythical "better mousetrap" to beat the competition. Just because he's not pencil pushing all day long doesn't mean he's wasting his time or the company's. It could be a costly mistake for the efficiency expert to recommend that this man's desk be moved to a windowless corner of the office where there's only a file cabinet for him to stare at.

Dreamers can be as unpopular in a modern setting as Joseph was with his brothers in ancient times. But a wise manager has to protect their window rights if there's some evidence of profitable creativity going on.

Another personality example is the woman who is all business every minute. She can be caricatured as having a phone cradled on each shoulder while she operates a word processor with one hand and a postage meter with the other. She is efficient with a capital "E," and the time and motion study people call her Wonder Woman. Her hourly work output intimidates everybody else in the office. She purses her lips and frowns a lot, especially at the man staring out the window!

A manager might raise several questions about this woman. Is her spectacular performance a reasonable standard for others? Is she possibly overworked? Is she a candidate for early burn-out? Does she need a diversion or an even bigger challenge or some kind of reward?

The basic consideration is that she must not be taken for granted or automatically categorized, simply because she's super satisfactory. Knowing that she tends to be a workaholic does not justify a supervisor in overloading her. To how much she does, and how well she does it, a people-centered employer will add a thought of what the job is doing to the woman.

In a large business, of course, the personnel department can address such concerns through its screening interviews and other means. But in considering management trainee prospects, especially, the supervisor should get personally involved and not rely only on references from others.

In fact, without obnoxious invasion of privacy, a manager should get to know something about an employee's family, living environment, personal interests, and social activities. All of these factors contribute significant drives to a person's character, and consequently to job conduct.

Yet another consideration that cannot be overlooked if workers are to be happy with their jobs is the way management conveys to them what they are asked to convey to others. Take that desk clerk again for an example. It's one thing to *order* him or her to be courteous to a customer, it's another to *help* them to be courteous. A manager must respect them as individuals and accord them the same courtesy, understanding, patience, and helpfulness that he or she wants extended in the company's behalf to its patrons.

After all, employees are quite likely to treat others the way they themselves are treated. If the boss shows personal interest in them, they are more likely to take a warm interest in the people they meet. Also, if they get the finest treatment in the world at the place where they work, they will feel their best on the job and will want to convey that sense of happiness to others.

Employees who believe management values their abilities and cares for their interests are bound to brag on the company when they're off the job, too, and thus advance its public drawing power.

All of this rationale behind the maxim "Be courteous" was written right into the operating manual of the Holiday Inn system for every innkeeper and supervisor to read and implement. The Attitude can never be taken for granted. It must be spelled out and hammered home constantly and consistently, by precept and by example.

Because local Holiday Inns employees across the United States felt they were valuable members of the corporate family, the same spirit took over that we experience in our homes whenever company's coming. Not only the innkeeper and the clerks at the front desk, but also the maids and housekeepers, the waitresses and bus boys, the yard men and janitors, the cooks and dishwashers—all took pride in welcoming our guests with friendly hospitality and in extending them attentive treatment during their stay.

Don't we all do the same when we entertain honored visitors in our own homes? The Holiday Inn family easily understood our Attitude, because we expressed it to each of them, personally and repeatedly. Every job assignment at an inn had the intrinsic dignity of being necessary, and the person who performed it had a corresponding sense of self-worth that was confirmed from the management level.

Don Loss is a good example of this. At the time he was president of the International Association of Holiday Inns, he invited me to address the annual awards banquet at his Perrysburg, Ohio, inn. I'd no sooner arrived and checked in, when Don asked me to go into the kitchen with him.

"I want to introduce you to someone, Bill. She's a lady in her sixties who has been working for me here in the same job for eleven years, without missing a day. I'd like you to say hello to her."

He guided me over to the area where the pots and pans were scrubbed and scalded. Patting the busy woman on her shoulder, he said, "Mary, I want to introduce you to Bill Walton. He's president of Holiday Inns."

She turned around with an expression of disbelief on her face.

"You're the president?" she asked.

"Yes, Mary, I am. Do you realize how important your job is? We spend millions of advertising dollars every year to encourage people to eat in our restaurants. You know what would happen if these pots and pans were not cleaned properly, and someone got sick from food poisoning! All our money and efforts would be wasted. What you do for us here is really valuable, and I want to say thank you for your eleven years of loyal help to your company. God bless you, dear."

Maybe it was the soapsuds that made her eyes suddenly brim.

"Mr. Walton," she said, "nobody has ever said a nicer thing to me." She gave me a spontaneous hug around the neck.

Don Loss had the Attitude. He knew, too, that no matter how good it looks on paper in the company charter, it's meaningless until it gets communicated to the people directly.

Happy people ordinarily make good producers, and consequently they don't have to worry much about holding onto their jobs. We had a man with us at Holiday Inns who had spent the previous forty years in the restaurant business.

He told me, "I never went home at night without a knot in my stomach, because I wondered if I'd have a job the next morning. At Holiday Inns, for the first time in my career, I feel I can be sure of my job, as long as I do it well."

That man was good for the company, because our attitude toward him made him happy on the job. And that's not just my personally biased perception.

In 1961, the editor of the *Journal of American Innkeeping,* Jim Pearson, came up from Jacksonville, Florida, to look over this strange outfit known as Holiday Inns, Inc. He ended up doing a twenty-four-page feature study of the company in the August issue. Concerning the spirit of the people who worked at Holiday City, he observed: "They include some men who used to look defeated but now look like schoolboys newly chosen for the varsity team. They look loaded with faith and hope, and I had heard about it and didn't understand it, and that's why I went there to find out about it."

The Rodney Dangerfields of this world who "don't get no respect" are more laughed with than at, I'd wager. It's not a pretty position to be in, especially if you have to be in it five days a week to earn a living.

Executives who want to achieve excellence in their management of a business, therefore, will have to start right at that point of making their people happy by showing consideration and respectful appreciation.

An excellent manager has the wisdom to know that building employee morale builds good business. It's that simple.

# 2. Creating Incentives
## *Do the People Feel Satisfied?*

A former treasurer of the American Olympics Committee once observed, "You've got to tell 'em to sell 'em, and you've got to see 'em to tell 'em."

We at the management level believed that we had to stay in direct touch with our people at Holiday Inns if we were going to be able to convey to them convincingly that we appreciated their best efforts on the company's behalf. To motivate people you need to go beyond the casual compliments and the policy considerations that give them a good feeling about themselves and their work.

While we wanted that sort of thing to happen every day on the local level, we dreamed up an annual occasion to do it officially in a way that would provide incentive for everybody to strive continually to realize their best potential.

The awards banquet at the franchisees' conference developed into an extravaganza to rival the best Oscar celebration Hollywood might produce!

It began modestly enough on May 25, 1956, when we brought to Memphis the current two dozen franchisees to meet with us at the home office in what was to become an annual meeting. I realized immediately and announced to the group that the next year our meeting would have to include the innkeepers as well. I felt that this was absolutely essential in order for those who were most directly responsible at the local level for personal treatment of our guests to identify with management's concerns.

The idea would be to portray to innkeepers their ultimate importance to the growth and success of the infant
Holiday Inns system. To encourage pride in a job well done
and a little friendly competition, we set up some criteria for
selecting the outstanding inn of the year, along with the outstanding innkeeper and assistant innkeeper (who was generally the restaurant manager). Always, you can be sure, demonstration of the Attitude was a fundamental judging point!

In later years, this simple contest was considerably expanded to include, for instance, the most innovative inn of
the year, the inn with the best maintenance and repair program, and the modernization award. To spread the recognition even further, we duplicated the entire awards structure
throughout the system by grouping inns according to size
and geographical region.

At each annual meeting we spared no effort or expense
to make the awards banquet memorable. Despite some executive pressure on me to stick to an all-American menu of
hamburgers and fries, I insisted that we put on a real seven-
course feast, with a live orchestra playing background music! The banquet room was suitably decorated, and the platform was designed to be a focus of attention.

The reason behind this fussiness about details was very
simple to me: we were gathering to honor people, and that
could hardly be the message we would send if the arrangements were second-rate.

The same principle applied to the awards themselves. It
wasn't enough just to call the winners up to the platform
to receive a handshake and a backslap from the chair of the
board, though that moment in the spotlight was worth a
lot in itself. I believed that an award needed tangible expression. We handed out such things as trophies, cash, free trips,
and Holiday Inns stock.

In the motivational speech of the evening, which usually fell to my lot, I stressed that there was no fun like being the best! Mediocrity, I told them, was within anybody's reach. We at Holiday Inns, by contrast, were stretching for excellence so that we could become number one. In a relatively few years, we did just that.

Not as ambitious as the annual system banquet, but just as significant, was the annual company banquet. This was a white-glove-and-champagne affair where the employees at Holiday City, our home base, received their service pins and other recognition.

This lapel pin, a miniature of the Holiday Inn Great Sign, was first given to employees when they had been with the company for three years. After five years, each year's pin had a jewel in it, ranging from an emerald for five years to a diamond for twenty-five. Such honoring of longevity with the company helped to make a lot of workers want to stay with us as long as they could.

Some of my executive associates recommended to me that we could save a lot of time at the banquet if we'd eliminate the parade of individuals across the platform and just have them all stand together and then pick up their pins back at the office from their department supervisor. You can imagine how receptive I was to that counsel! That, to me, is not recognition but mere formality.

Our biggest annual event, though, was not the awards banquet at the franchisees' meeting or the company banquet. It was family day at Holiday City, the corporate headquarters on Lamar Avenue in Memphis. The last time I was involved with it, we estimated that 10,000 attended, including employees and their spouses and children.

The eighty-five-acre corporate campus was transformed for the occasion into a veritable fairgrounds! Rides, cotton candy, games, balloons, and all kinds of prizes for every imaginable category of people.

Every member of the headquarters work force was encouraged to bring the whole family to see where mother or daddy worked. It was mandatory for all management personnel and officers of the company to be there, mingling throughout the day with the whole crowd.

Part of the event was open house in all departments and offices. That didn't leave out the executive suite sanctum of chairman, president, and others. For most of the workers themselves, it was their only occasion to ascend to the rarified atmosphere of the fourth floor. But everybody also took spouse and children to their own work area and explained what they did there each day while away from home.

It's my personal persuasion that a lot of marital and family troubles arise from ignorance about what occupies the breadwinner at the place of work each day during those long hours of absence from the house. Knowledge + Understanding = Acceptance. We couldn't make a big deal about being the "Holiday Inn FAMILY" and then disregard the actual families of the people who worked for us.

Probably the favorite attraction on those family day outings was the miniature train in which children could ride all over the grounds—with its engineer, Chairman of the Board Kemmons Wilson, seeming to revel in the rides fully as much as his passengers did!

My greatest personal pleasure was to see the pride of workers when they came up to me and said, "Mr. Walton, I want you to meet my family!" I kissed babies and shook hands with little boys and girls and patted people on the head or shoulder as if I were a politician running for office—and I loved every minute of it!

How can employees feel they are known and understood if the company they work for treats their off-the-job relationships, especially with family, as nonexistent? The Attitude of excellence in management has got to respect the whole context of an individual worker's life, without intrusion, of course, but with sincere interest.

At the same time, the family at home can become more supportive of the wage earner when it knows what the job involves. The linkage between home and job is a strong incentive to workers in itself, because they want their loved ones to be proud of their accomplishments at work, and it strengthens the bonds of belonging without which neither family nor company can prosper completely.

Naturally, there are far less grandiose ways than those annual flings to create incentives that motivate people's top performance on the job. I never knew when some seemingly minor message emanating from headquarters would draw an employee response.

In a Thanksgiving letter to the Holiday Inn family one November, I wrote, "I am thankful that we have never become 'too big' to be nice to the public."

A few days later, I received a note from the assistant restaurant manager at an inn in Milwaukee that said, "We, in turn, are grateful that the heads of our large family have not become too big to bestow that always appreciated pat on the back, showing that our efforts have not gone unnoticed."

A company of people is not simply a conglomerate. It is in the deepest sense a corporation. What a rich word that is, suggesting the metaphor of a body, a compatible group of individually different but mutually dependent members. A living organism, in fact.

That's why the motivational necessity laid on management cannot be fulfilled with occasional morale-building gestures. It is absolutely imperative that there be a steady pulsing of incentives moving through that body of workers on a daily basis.

It's not enough to compliment a worker on bed-making technique. It's not even enough to greet the spouse at a picnic and tickle a baby under the chin.

If such persons are to feel that their work as members of the business family is rewarding, they need to know that they can render a service to company associates as well as fill a job in the work force. It is not a decision-making role that affects research and development, to be sure. But it's something more important than slipping an item into the employees' suggestion box, which seldom gets emptied in a lot of offices!

Workers should be given every encouragement to add the gifts of their unique personalities to the mix of people they work with every day. Maybe a man is a listener. Lots of people could be healed of anxieties and pains if they could just find a listener.

Or maybe a woman is a problem solver, with the not-so-common sense to objectify and analyze difficulties that others are facing.

Maybe some are gifted with that rare commodity, cheerfulness—not just irrepressible optimism but a genuine ability to find a bright side and help balance the picture.

"Well and good," some griper may interject, "but what do they know about the Dow averages?"

Nothing, perhaps. They may have only an eighth-grade education. Yet life experience and the good Lord may have given the wisdom of a Solomon. What does it matter that they can't explain a sudden stock market decline, as long as they can point the way to riding it out emotionally?

When you stop to think that fellow workers spend more

consecutive hours each day with each other than with their family and friends, it should be obvious that they are at least positioned to be very helpful to each other beyond the minimum job requirements. Managerial excellence recognizes this diversity of gifts and their wholesome impact on the corporate family, and it fosters their use.

After all, is there any solid reason to suppose that the rank and file in our companies are lesser people simply because their credentials are minimal and their assignments may be menial? Leaders who recognize that all individuals in the company have support-building strengths will find their own excellence enhanced by readily drawing on such gifts.

Because I felt keenly the need for all the help I could get from the first day that Kemmons Wilson and Wallace Johnson asked me to put together a corporation and franchise system for Holiday Inns, I made it a practice to invite headquarters staff people to sit in with us at board meetings, even with the executive committee. I don't know any stronger incentive for rising young managerial staff to put their best foot forward than to throw them into the arena with the powers that be.

But I had to fight for that privilege on their behalf! It seems that some directors of corporations assume they've risen to the top because they're the cream. Apparently, they're no longer supposed to mix with common milk. Well, I homogenized those meetings!

It wasn't done so that staff could intrude into board deliberations. But they deserved to know first-hand what was going on at the company policymaking level that would have an effect on their departments. That way they could provide expert insights, when called on from time to time, to help the board reach workable decisions.

Didn't that make for some long board meetings? You

bet! I wouldn't have it any other way. We met one Saturday a month, for all day. If a member didn't want to give it that kind of time, he could sit on another board, as far as I was concerned.

This was the procedure we followed for fifteen years or so. No one-hour rubber stamping of executive committee recommendations the way it was done in a lot of the board meetings I heard about in other organizations. Not only did this contribute to the necessary self-esteem of administrative department heads, but it kept open the all-important channels of communication between executive and middle management.

I guess I was lucky to win these concessions as long as I did. The time came, even while I was president, that board meeting time was cut back to once a quarter for an hour and a half or less, with nonmember attendance severely restricted; and the chairman took a more aggressive role in conducting the sessions than had been his custom until then.

I'm sure those younger people who were excluded found their jobs considerably less rewarding after they lost this chance to observe top management's deliberations. Whether it was cause and effect I can't say, but unrest or outright dissatisfaction began to mar the boardroom proceedings, too, as valuable input was lost. A lot of negative factors were combining to cause it, but I remain convinced that a major one was the curtailment of open communication.

Failure to communicate amounts to one party telling another, "You don't need to know, and I don't have to tell you what's going on in my area." That's demeaning to the one who is cut off, and it is bound to foment hard feelings. A company of loners is bound to be a loser.

The stockholders' annual meeting was another ideal occasion for me to parade the people of Holiday Inns. I used to invite anyone who wished to sit in. Time permitting, I'd introduce the leaders to the crowd: "I'm very proud of So-and-So, vice-president of such-and-such division, and of the job these people have done this year. I welcome this chance to introduce them to you." Then I'd have members of the department or division who were present stand up and take a bow.

When those meetings adjourned, we'd serve coffee and doughnuts, and I'd encourage company people to mix with stockholders, introduce themselves, and describe their company activities.

How many major corporations today give their stockholders even a glimpse of the people really responsible for those dividends they all are so eager to receive? The main objective seems to be to get out in an hour, even avoiding stockholders' questions as much as possible or referring them to a public relations officer or a department representative for an answer later in private. The opportunity for communication and camaraderie is forfeited completely in favor of minimal adherence to legal requirements.

Such is the fallacy of business administration theory today: in the name of efficiency, punch the computer keys and let human relations be damned. Those who search for excellence have shown conclusively that such a spirit is the antithesis to what has historically accounted for greatness in America's leading companies. Those that abandoned people in favor of a printout are not on the list of excellent companies compiled by researchers like Peters, Naisbitt, Kennedy, and others. Nor are they generally noted for ever-rising performance standards and production records. When the true "company" is forgotten, or forfeited, the business machine begins to run out of steam.

The whole history of trade unionism in this country illustrates the point. The moguls of industry at the dawning of the age of machines forgot about people. The mechanization of production via the assembly line made mere cogs of men and women. Talk about killing incentive! It's no wonder there was protest and riot and bloodshed on the labor front. Working people justifiably want their needs to be noticed, and unions were their answer to cavalier management attitudes.

I admit to bragging that in my years in management at Holiday Inns, Inc., we never lost one of some 200-plus union elections. Well, we did lose one in Pascagoula, Mississippi, with the Teamsters union that we inherited along with our acquisition of Delta Steamship Company and the Continental Trailways Bus Company. The next year, though, we came back and won that one, too!

My bragging is not because we beat the unions. It's because we demonstrated to our people that the benefits and advantages of working at Holiday Inns already surpassed anything the unions could promise to do for them.

My message was simple and to the point:

"You don't need a union to pressure your company to do what is right and fair for you and to recognize the dignity of your position. Your company has a history of doing that which is in the best interest of its people through generous benefits, salary scales, retirement programs, and advancement opportunities. The company attitude is one of doing the utmost for you, keeping in mind the need to protect the financial stability of your company and to continue its progress. Our attitude over the years has placed you first in the company's sense of responsibility."

The people at Holiday Inns knew I was not trying to defraud them. Companies lose union elections because the company people have learned to their great sorrow that they can't trust management to deliver on its promises. They don't believe what management says because the attitudes of management are so obviously contradictory. The added dimension of excellence that cares about people is missing.

In fact, I was shocked when I first encountered the subsidiary management attitudes in the Trailways strike. I never before had heard executives use such disrespectful language toward their work force. Not only did they not seem to care about the concerns of their laborers, they were actually contemptuous of them.

Of course their people went on strike and stayed on strike for nearly a year. In the meeting between Holiday Inns executives and the top level managers of the bus company, I really lost my cool and proceeded to tell them off in language probably just as strong as they had been using!

My own chairman made it perfectly clear that he didn't like my conduct at that meeting. His partner, Wallace, didn't support me in the meeting itself but phoned me in my office later and said, "Hooray for you!"

A close look at the bus company earnings back then should give adequate evidence that a hard-nosed management attitude toward legitimate labor concerns doesn't pay in the long haul. I think such companies are prostituting their people, taking advantage of them in an uncaring manner.

If business and industry in this country are going to experience the turnaround everybody so ardently wants and regain the respect and trade of the world market, they'll not get far or last long at it by depriving their own workers of incentives.

After all, it's my conviction—often tested and confirmed—that people are much more responsive to a hugging than to a mugging! Let employees know that you respect their innate human worth and that you value their talents, and you'll usually find that they will go out of their way to give you a satisfactory performance in what's required of them.

One of the little things that took place at the very beginning of the adventure of Holiday Inns perhaps sums up what I've been trying to emphasize about the Attitude of caring for people as the bedrock of management excellence.

Our first Christmas as a full-scale business operation was fast approaching and we wanted to let those first valiant and visionary employees know that we really appreciated their casting in their lot with us. But we simply didn't have enough change in the company coffers to do anything for them.

So we sent each employee a personal note expressing our esteem and gratitude and explaining the company's financial situation. But our "Merry Christmas" didn't stop with that. We also enclosed an I.O.U. for $25 as our Christmas gift, promising that as soon as we could—within six months, if possible—we would redeem those notes.

We did.

Attitude may be an elusive concept to define, but it's not at all hard to demonstrate. And unless the attitude of management about motivating the people who make up the company is a good one, backed by strong compensation and incentive plans, morale will plummet. If executives think they can leave the issue of company morale to the public relations department, they will have a disaster on their hands.

I have always been grateful for the good counsel I received early in our business experience at Holiday Inns from the senior partner of a leading public relations firm in New

York. We wanted to hire their services to put us on the right track. The gray-haired gentleman representing them startled me with his opening salvo as he sat with me in my office.

"Mr. Walton," he began, "may I say this at the outset. If you have a pile of manure here that you want to hire me and my firm to whitewash, we are not interested. On the other hand, if you recognize that yours is the responsibility for developing morale and attitude within your company, and ours will simply be the job of communicating it, then you will find us to be the best in the business."

There's no doubt about it: top management is responsible for morale. Not just to advocate it, or even to program it, but to induce it by example. That's ultimately the most influential incentive.

By contrast, I don't know of anything more destructive to good spirit among employees than managers modeling immorality, deceitfulness, lack of trustworthiness, failure to face unpleasant issues, back stabbing, favoritism, nest feathering, and pushing selfish goals at the expense of one's associates.

At our staff meetings I made a speech every so often that went something like this: "If you want my job, I want you to have it. If you are willing to commit yourself and dedicate yourself to those things necessary to do my job and to pull yourself up by your own bootstraps, I will congratulate you and help you. On the other hand, I have no tolerance for back stabbing, dishonesty, drunkenness, and promiscuity. If you're ever caught doing things like that, I can assure you of a quick ticket out of Holiday Inns."

Those were one-way tickets, and I issued them on several occasions!

In the matter of motivation, every company has to discipline as well as reward employees. Sometimes work performance just isn't up to par. As an executive, I'd be a hypocrite to compliment someone for a poor job.

Under such circumstances, can you still keep the incentive pulse beating? Here's how I tried. On the premise that humiliation and ridicule did not express our caring Attitude, I usually started out by saying, "Let's talk about this situation," or, "What do you think?"

I might go on to ask if the goal we had set was too high to reach. Very few times did anyone want to say yes to that. Instead, they usually would reaffirm the goal, reevaluate their previous approach to it, and then pledge to personally work harder to achieve it. A respectful demeanor in the manager, even when he or she is displeased, can do a lot to help motivate improved performance thereafter.

Many executives touch and influence the lives of thousands of people, both inside and outside the company. Their touch can be a blight or a blessing. Their influence can build up a person or tear down. To have a positive impact, they need to set the prime example of honesty, loyalty, dedication, and sincere caring.

Old-fashioned virtues? No question about that. But the need for demonstrating them in the business community today is critical. In one recent national survey on values, business people were next to the bottom of the scale (just above politicians!) as those least respected by the general populace. What a scandal for a country that prides itself on the free enterprise system!

Executive Attitude. How management views and treats people. It's where excellence begins. Or ends. A rotten attitude at the top will make the whole company stink!

With the right Attitude, though, management can handle

a lot of the inevitable day-to-day difficulties of running a business and still come out smelling like the proverbial rose.

Even more importantly, with the right Attitude management can motivate workers by pointing beyond problems to possibilities. As one of the company's senior vice-presidents, John Greene, explained a few years ago, the reason we shipped our standard eighty-inch-long double beds to furnish the new Kyoto Inn was our confidence that over the next fifty years the Japanese will get taller!

When it comes to motivating people, there's no incentive more powerful than executive exuberance!

# 3. Offering Benefits
## *Do the People Feel Rewarded?*

Banquets and picnics are lots of fun, but they could be just empty gestures or window dressing—public relations ploys to simulate rather than stimulate company spirit. The corporation has to put its money where its mouth is if it's going to motivate its people. It must develop tangible plans to enhance employee relations in substantial ways that go beyond emotional or programmatic morale boosters.

How does an excellent manager look out for people's best interests? Showing consideration can take different forms in different settings. But there's no getting around the fact that in a place where people work to earn a living to support their families, consideration has to go beyond compliments to compensation—spelled C-A-S-H.

I heard a story about the chairperson of a meeting saying afterwards to the guest speaker, "Oh, I don't know how we can ever thank you." The speaker replied, "Ever since the Phoenicians invented money, there's been only one way."

You simply cannot substitute thanks for cash. And you can't pay in promises. People depend on an adequate paycheck. If it's not forthcoming, their morale can't be pumped up by any other effort.

It was always a cardinal principle with us to pay fair wages. I think we met the competition and exceeded it in supplemental benefits. But how any employer defines that term *fair* can be challenged, and there are sure to be some grumblers in the work force who are never satisfied with what you do for them.

It was my responsibility as chief operating officer for twenty years to represent the wage issue to the chief executive officer. We were not unionized, of course, and I did everything in my power to advocate the people's case. There, as in all other business matters, it was "win a few, lose a few." On the whole, though, I think I usually came away from the tussle with a pay scale everybody could live with.

If employers approach the wage question by asking how much they can get out of the people for how little, they are likely to stir up some real problems with the work force, motivational and otherwise. Think of the damage done to employee attitudes toward the job if they get the idea that management is insensitive to their financial needs.

This can become particularly sticky if company decision makers aren't following a carefully wrought scale that takes into account such elements as seniority, grades of job difficulty, stages of advancement, and so forth. For all the emphasis we put on relating to workers *personally*, I had to see to it that we did not base compensation on an *individual* basis. There had to be guidelines and standards that were equitable for all.

If great care is not taken to see that workers at each level are receiving a fair day's pay for a day's work, one or more things can happen to employee attitude.

1. Attitude toward the company will be poor because those who perceive themselves as underpaid will feel they are being exploited. This becomes increasingly true among advanced positions where performance expectations generally run higher and noncompensated overtime can become

the rule rather than the exception. I can recall one exasperated officer one time yelling at his people: "Let's try some 100-hour work weeks!" Had that actually happened, no adjustments likely would have showed up in their paychecks, and the workers would not have felt happy about the situation, to say the least!

It isn't always the intrinsic wage figure that matters as much as the psychological impact on workers and their families. Whenever a working father or mother has to say to the children, "We can't afford that," it has the potential to raise an image of the employer as a tight-fisted Scrooge.

2. Attitude toward fellow workers deteriorates. They ask themselves why some associate who has no greater responsibility than theirs seems to get a better deal from the company.

This is the stuff on which envy and jealousy feed, and those emotions are exceedingly detrimental to good morale. Beyond that, if inequitable compensation generates ill will among peers, they are quite likely to stop taking initiative to help one another.

3. Attitude toward their immediate superior in a department or division is critically affected. Assuming that the superior knows best what responsibility and performance standards are for a given job, an employee can logically assume also that the superior is responsible for wage evaluations. If compensation doesn't match responsibility, it might be seen as the superior's fault, and she or he risks losing both respect and loyalty.

The superior's own status could suffer, furthermore, because the aggrieved employee might assume that the manager has limited authority: the power to require but not to reward.

4. Attitude of supervisory employees similarly becomes

tense toward the employees they are responsible to oversee. Since supervisors have little or no voice in determining how to compensate them in proportion to their work load, supervisors probably would be reluctant to ask their workers to increase productivity. After all, what's the incentive? What can a supervisor promise that they can look forward to? It's cold comfort to hard workers to be told that maybe next time they will be paid what they've earned.

I know that this all sounds very negative, but I'm afraid that experience has taught me it is not the natural impulse of employers to be generous with the people who work for them when it comes to wages. An excellent executive, committed to thinking right about motivating people, cannot afford to overlook the financial component of the Attitude.

An employer who is lavish with praise but stingy with money is going to have employee morale and motivation problems. Company loyalty is undermined, work output is reduced, employee energy is diverted to planning how to offset the salary shortfall, and eventually the lure of greener pastures with some other business draws them away.

Executives owe it to themselves and to the corporation, as well as to their employees, to establish policies and procedures respecting wages that are truly fair. I can only reiterate that a right Attitude of excellence is the best safeguard against demoralizing discrimination and exploitation. No company officer who controls the purse strings should ever use that trust as a club over an employee's head. It is self-defeating to put profit above people.

In addition to wage considerations, so-called fringe benefits are pretty standard throughout business and industry employment contracts. That, also, is not necessarily because employers are altruistic, I'm afraid, but more often because minimal decency drove them to it as a last resort. Provisions like vacation time, sick leave, hospital insurance—hardly anyone dares deny these to workers anymore. More generous programs may go as far as credit unions, continuing education, stock options, and profit sharing.

I get a lot of satisfaction out of knowing that we put together a really distinguished program at Holiday Inns, Inc. All of the above were part of our package, along with many other benefits.

It wasn't that easy, however, to get some of them approved and implemented. The axiom "Charity begins at home" isn't a favorite motto in many executive offices. How little a company can get by with doing for its employees is a more conventional principle. That's a wrong attitude toward people, and it's the opposite of managerial excellence, which never rests with what's standard, but always presses on to something better.

When I began to explore the possibilities of instituting an employee profit-sharing plan, I turned to the noble example of one of the biggest of them all, Sears Roebuck, and practically copied the page out of their book. That company was a true pacesetter in taking care of its employees.

Before I borrowed from them, though, I had asked for a draft plan from a sophisticated Chicago personnel firm. When I saw their proposal, I told them it wouldn't do for Holiday Inns. We wanted a plan that would include John the yard man.

"You can't do that," the Chicago executive told me.

That's usually about all it takes to rouse my contrariness. So I walked out on the experts and simply drew up a plan for us that *does* include John the yard man. No problem!

How it worked to the advantage of employees is abundantly documented. For example, at the end of the first eight years of operation, participating employees numbered

13,000. Plan assets stood at $18 million, with half of that from company contributions. The return on contributions made by an employee who had been there from the beginning ranged from 680% to 1100%.

I don't know where John the yard man ranked in those percentages, but I do know that as the years passed, many employees were able to buy nice homes, put children through college, and accumulate substantial supplemental retirement resources through the benefits of profit-sharing and stock option programs.

I can't underscore it too strongly: the right Attitude toward people is simply caring about them. Management's motivation for a suitable employee benefits program has to be response to identifiable needs, not just bare accommodation to some list of abstract specifications drawn up by statisticians.

Jimmy Durante used to sing, "The song's gotta come from da heart!" It's the same way with caring. You can't put it on and take it off at will, like a mask. It's either *in* you or it's fraud.

For a few years we sponsored a group of marvelous young people called "The Messengers." They went all over the world representing the company and our ideals. Their theme song, which opened our annual meetings and often introduced my appearance at the dedication of new inns, was: "Do You Really Care?" That was our message, without a doubt.

This caring for employees can translate into intensely personal terms. Around Christmas 1958, shortly after we had moved into our new offices on Lamar Avenue, the Shelby County sheriff's deputy showed up in our accounting department one day to serve a garnishment on the salary of one of our Holiday Inn people. When someone passed the word to my office, I was infuriated that this would be done only a day or two before Christmas. Talk about the ghost of Ebenezer Scrooge!

Storming into the middle of the situation, I denounced the move in terms hardly appropriate to the season, notified the authority that current salary checks had already been issued, and succeeded in thwarting the unhappy action for the moment.

That crisis made me realize that many of our people were victims of high interest rates, and worse—of downtown loan sharks. The Attitude factor prompted me to institute some immediate steps to relieve them.

Within the year, therefore, we proceeded to set up an employees' credit union, supported by the company, which came to be known as the Holiday Inn Savings and Loan Association. I called a meeting of our workers and explained that this was their organization, through which they could borrow at favorable terms to buy the things they needed.

Also, because our expansion had driven us to develop many supply sources and subsidiary operations, we arranged for our employees to do family shopping at advantageous prices in some of our own warehouses, a prototype of the company store that is not too uncommon with manufacturers today. At Innkeepers Supply, for instance, they could buy such things as carpeting, drapes, television sets, household furnishings, and small appliances, for cost–plus–5%–plus–freight and a 10% deposit (not to exceed $50).

They could even buy discounted tickets for various recreational and amusement opportunities in the community through the Employee Benefit Office. We also made arrangements for Holiday Inns employees to get special consideration on prices from some of the cooperating showrooms and dealerships with which we did company business, including automobile agencies.

Actions like these all said to our people more loudly than words: Management cares about you and wants you to be a real member of the corporate family.

That spirit, understandably, doesn't coexist too comfortably with a system of executive perks that reserves special privileges and favors for a small elitist clique of leaders! I found that out myself.

I thoroughly enjoyed the benefits that came to me as chief operating officer, benefits that few others in the company could experience. Having a Learjet at my disposal twenty-four hours a day, for instance. We could hardly make that available to every worker to take the family on a free vacation to an inn on the Riviera!

But executives readily fall into a mindset that expects, and then demands, unusual advantages as their rightful due, whether the responsibility of their office justifies them or not. While there are definite and legitimate levels of privilege that go with corresponding degrees of official obligation, the danger is in establishing an executive aristocracy and thus impairing or destroying the sense of "company."

The various efforts a business makes, therefore, to benefit its people, from typist to tycoon, should be appropriate without being ostentatious. Chances are, for example, that no one actually deserves the parking space nearest to the front door, so why make a big deal over putting some officer's name on it? If anything, assign it to the employee of the month as part of company recognition for exceptional service. A trivial concession? Yes. But a powerful message.

What I've been describing as illustrative benefits to our employees, designed to help make them feel that it was worth seeking and holding a job at Holiday Inns, Inc., have become widely adopted over the years in the business community. But one program we instituted was not only different, it was radical at the time.

That was the Chaplaincy, both at the company, and in the system through a Chaplain-on-Call program.

Did we ever get the reactions to that! One typical protest came from the minister of a large church in Nevada: "Why is Holiday Inns trying to start a church? We want no part in a program of watered-down, motel religion!"

That may have been one of the gentler indictments.

But think about it. We had overtly stated many times over since our founding that "respect for the dignity of the individual, and the Christian principle of man's love for his fellowman" were our guiding philosophy. Kemmons and Wallace and I were all affiliated with churches and agreed together about the spiritual dimension being a part of company character.

In no way did we ever conceive of Holiday Inns getting into the religion business. That was the prerogative of churches and synagogues. But within the boundaries of our day-to-day business operations, we knew, many situations arose where employees needed counsel that went beyond the vocational or psychological.

What the chaplaincy did was to reinforce our commitment to the Attitude in practical ways that employees could identify with at times of special need in their lives. The Reverend W. A. (Dub) Nance, who founded the program for us, did perform pastoral functions for employees when called on—weddings, funerals, christenings, and the like—because many did not have a regular church of their own. But that was really a very minor aspect of his service to the company. A typical report from his office might include the following:

11 employees counseled intensively for 15 hours
31 employees visited in hospitals
2 bereaved employees visited
2 weddings for Holiday Inn employees
4 office meetings with families of alcoholics
14 church directories prepared for inns
4 hours of classes taught at Holiday Inn University
4 executive prayer breakfasts conducted
672 incoming phone calls received
8 Inns supplied with Gideon Bibles

That's only part of one month's report, which also included sending personal letters in behalf of my office to 104 students at the university, 20 congratulatory messages, 35 get well wishes, and 20 expressions of sympathy.

Caring for our people. That's all it was.

And sometimes, sadly, a situation was tragic. In a memo to me about the suicide of a twenty-two-year-old male employee, Dub lamented the fact that we had no advance indications that enough desperation lay hidden within to drive the man to self-destruction. So far as we knew, he and his supervisor got along well in the work situation, and he could have gone on happily there indefinitely. Personal problems never came into his discussions with anyone. His wife was also employed with us, and she gave no indication that she knew her husband was troubled to such an intolerable extent.

You can't always win. On the other hand, from inns in the system and from the local ministers who voluntarily served them as Chaplain-on-Call, the very opposite kind of story came in not infrequently. There was the case of a $65,000-per-year executive who had lost his job and had gone to a Holiday Inn to take his life. Dr. Gordon Clarke, one of our volunteers, hurried to the Inn, where he talked the man out of suicide and took him home to his wife.

According to some of our estimates, an average of 500 inn guests each year did that kind of turnaround through a chaplain's influence—or the presence of an open Gideon Bible in their room.

In another typical instance, a traveler received word while staying at an inn that her daughter had been killed in an auto accident. One of our chaplains was at her side at once with the comfort her own pastor was not present to give. If trouble doesn't ride with travelers, it chases them.

A letter from a man in La Jolla, California, was representative of thousands we received over the years:

> During mid-June, I was a guest at Holiday Inn Northeast in San Antonio. I was facing a most serious personal crisis and turned to the chaplain for the inn. I consider that the Reverend L. saved my life and turned me in a new direction. . . ."

An innkeeper in Ontario received a report from one of the local ministers who volunteered to be "on call" with this upbeat commentary:

> We are glad to say that not all of the calls, by any means, are of a critical or tragic nature. For example, several people take the opportunity to phone simply to say how delighted they are to know that there are corporations that think in terms of people's spiritual needs. Others phone simply to have a chat, having arrived from across the Atlantic or across the Pacific for a few days on business, and

just to share in a friendly conversation. Others are quite lonely and are so glad to have someone who is available simply to come and have coffee and conversation.

All of that kind of response seemed to me to validate the BENEFIT that the chaplain program was to employees and guests of Holiday Inns. But it was contested constantly within the executive suite by some officers who, as soon as their chance came to exercise the authority, dismantled the whole program and dismissed the company chaplain as well. I'll have more to say about this dimension of Holiday Inns activity later, but two other testimonials are appropriate at this point.

First, from an innkeeper in Buffalo, New York:

> My experience in the motel field has shown me this is a much-needed program, and probably will help eliminate some of the day-to-day problems each and every innkeeper encounters. On a number of occasions I have found myself discussing guests' personal problems. It seems it is easier for them to talk to a stranger . . . The program has my full endorsement.

Second, appearing in a London, England, newspaper report from a journalist visiting in the United States, under the caption "Bless This House, Inc.":

> The combination of God, Mammon, and hot buttered toast is one that was not uncommon in the flourishing business houses of Victorian England. In America, where the age of prosperity is not quite over, the happy partnership lingers on.
> It lingers on particularly here in Memphis where each Wednesday the president of Holiday Inns, Inc., William

Walton, sits down for coffee and devotions with the eighty or so top dogs of his hotel empire . . .

There was grace, and then there were scrambled eggs and English muffins, and then there were prayers. For a waitress in California with a sick husband. For a bereaved chambermaid in Denver. For a desk clerk awaiting an operation.

The man next to me whispered: "It shows them that we care. If we care about our staff, they will care about our guests."

The British reporter concluded:

"I expect in my flippant way I've given the impression that the whole thing was a hoot. In fact, I'm sure I was among good and worthy people, as I would have been long ago among the philanthropist woolmasters of Yorkshire who put up statues and opened reading-rooms for the poor."

I'll add just this footnote: How do you think we eighty "top dogs" at that prayer breakfast found out about the needs in the life of the California waitress and the Denver chambermaid and the ill desk clerk? *They* let us know, because they believed that the executives in Memphis meant it when they said, "We care."

Undoubtedly, one of the primary forces behind the development of Holiday Inns, Inc., was the Attitude. A combination of love for neighbor, mutual self-help, and cooperation, it drew its strength and inspiration from the sound roots of religion. The chaplain program was instituted to preserve and expand the Attitude.

It was quite a parish Dub and his helpers served: 2,200 employees at Holiday City headquarters in Memphis, 150,000 employees in the worldwide system, and upwards of a quarter of a million inn guests each night.

I made no apologies then, and I make no apologies now, for "benefiting" our people with that program.

Right thinking about motivation of the company personnel cannot stop with stimulating the labor of their hands. It has to take their hearts into account, too.

A former chairman of Inland Steel, Clarence Randall, said:

"To be worthy of management responsibility today, a man must have an insight into the human heart. Unless he has an awareness of human problems, a sensitivity toward the hopes and aspirations of those whom he supervises, and a capacity for analysis of the emotional forces that motivate their conduct, the projects entrusted to him will not get ahead—no matter how often wages are raised."

It was Randall, also, who said that in all his years in the steel industry, he had never had to know anything about metallurgy, but everything about people.

Company officers who seclude themselves in their offices, or who only perform a stuffed-shirt strut on ceremonial occasions, cannot be motivators—and cannot claim excellence. Being in touch with the people, conveying the caring Attitude, is the indispensable criterion by which their managerial fitness and finesse will ultimately be judged.

# II. THINKING RIGHT ABOUT TRAINING PEOPLE

# 4. Giving Instruction
## Can the People Understand the Job?

Almost as far back as I can remember, I've been fascinated by the concept of training, helping people understand how to do a job well. In early childhood, I organized boys and girls in my home neighborhood to sell soft drinks from old baby buggies that they pushed along the scorching Memphis sidewalks on midsummer days.

In high school I ran my friend's election campaign for student government president by identifying the skills of various classmates, training committees, assigning jobs, outlining strategies, and staging a sensational student rally that woke up all the neighbors at seven in the morning.

When I went to work for the DuPont Company as a material control expediter about the time of World War II, I had to see that the right materials were at the right construction site at the right time every day as we built a vast munitions plant. This required me to understand not only what each laborer and tradesman were doing, but also the time sequence and job schedule. It bred in me a determination to help people know what to do and when and why—and I like to think that it helped that particular DuPont plant to earn the government's coveted "E" Award (for excellence!).

Then came my stint in the military service, in the Army Air Force. The day I was inducted as a volunteer, all my dreams of taking off with my high school buddies into the wide blue yonder crashed. Because I had already started working nights on my law degree, the military figured I should be an instructor of recruits at the base in Las Vegas.

Needless to say, I was exposed to some immediate intensive training myself, since the airmen under my instruction were only three or four years younger than I and were destined very quickly for heavy action on the battlefront.

Our country had not been building a war machine in those years prior to the Pearl Harbor attack, so in 1943 we still did not have well-organized training programs or any of the teaching aids we have since come to take for granted. I had to start almost from scratch designing devices to train those "boys" (most just out of high school) to develop a team spirit in mastering the fine points of the B-17 bomber, later starting all over again when the B-29 was introduced.

Over the continent of Europe and over the Pacific, lives hung in the balance daily as those aircraft went out on their missions. The boys inside those flying fortresses *had* to know what they were doing. I took my instructor assignment very seriously. Probably that service stint out in Nevada did more than anything else in my life up to that time to sell me on the absolute necessity of quality training.

So when the war was over, I came away from all of it with a lasting admiration for the value of organization: creating concepts of what needs to be done, conducting training programs on how to do it, motivating people to do it with efficiency, and compensating adequately for a job well done.

The need for training is analogous to a gusher in the oil fields. What good to anybody is that copious flow of black gold from the well until it is piped to storage tanks and distribution centers for eventual consumer use?

Motivation is like that gusher. By probing into a personality, you can find and release the driving force that has potential for producing tremendous results. But all the good Attitude toward people and the high hopes for their promise to be realized get nowhere without the pipeline of training.

It's not enough to get people *charged* up. You've got to get them *linked* up, too, both with the specific job you're asking them to do, and with other people who will join them in accomplishing it. Just to give locker room pep talks without signaling the plays out on the field is lousy strategy in athletics. The same principle holds true in running a business.

An excellent manager operates on the assumption that even the most gifted people need all the help they can get if they are to reach their maximum capability. A lot of brilliance and talent go to waste in the business world every day because people don't know how to apply their gifts to what they are assigned to do. If you care about people, you will recognize that channeling their abilities has to be the immediate follow-up to challenging them.

Modern business leaders could do a lot worse than to review the instructional approach of that one often referred to as the master teacher, Jesus of Nazareth, as depicted in the New Testament Gospels. Even a quick reading shows that he used such time-tested methods as theory and application, laboratory demonstration, apprenticeship and internship, field testing, and review and evaluation.

Given the right Attitude to start with, nothing is more important than training. Given a wrong attitude, though, no amount of training will be ultimately productive.

I am totally convinced that there can be no true managerial excellence apart from an unswerving dedication to training. Yet how many businesses initially place people, and subsequently promote them, without tending to their need for regularly up-dated instruction? That neglect undermines morale and reduces productivity.

Here again, it's management's expressed and demonstrated attitude about training that is the crucial factor in achieving excellence. But training can never be a substitute for motivation. The right Attitude about people, applied through the caring touch on their lives, must come first if training goals are to be accomplished.

This emphasis I keep repeating about a caring Attitude toward people makes a lot of business leaders nervous. They like to boast that they run people companies, and yet they're afraid to get too close to their workers.

While sense, not sentiment, has to guide executive actions, maybe one reason some managers work at keeping aloof from employees is that they fear any "warm, fuzzy feelings" will cloud their administrative judgment. Day-to-day business decisions are hard enough to make, they know, without getting emotionally involved. Besides, they reason, too much display of executive friendliness might breed insubordination and anarchy in the rank and file.

There's some truth to all of that. Certain people are quick to take advantage of any hint of softness in the boss. Sometimes personal attachments can dim discernment. Executives have to be careful to avoid both prejudice and preferment where employees are concerned.

It's wrong, though, to imply that sensible management is impaired by due respect for human individuality. That confuses the issue.

In the first place, sentimentality and feeling are not synonyms for respect. The latter can be based only on faith in a divine ideal about what it is to be a human, coupled with rock-hard experiential evidence. We have to commit ourselves to this Attitude in principle and then constantly put it to the test in practice. Looking for the best in people, out of respect for their Creator's intentions for their lives, is the very opposite of gullible softness.

In the second place, respect for individuality does not mean letting everyone do their own thing. The words *corporation* and *company* by definition mean a working association of people, doing *together* what they could not do as well on their own.

What managers are supposed to manage is not the people, however, but the joint *effort* of the people.

Given that fundamental respect for the strengths and skills of individual workers, then, excellence is further measured by the ability to coordinate tasks. Here is where training enters the picture—rigorous, demanding employee training. All workers must be thoroughly indoctrinated as to how their respective job duties and accomplishments relate to the whole operation and help to determine the outcome.

Employees need to know not only *how* to do well what they are assigned to do, but also *why* their doing it well can make a big difference between corporate failure or success.

We took pains to spell out concerns like that in the operating manual. It might be assumed, for instance, that check-in of guests should always be as expeditious as possible, without making them feel rushed. But why? We illustrated the consequence of an inefficient check-in this way:

"It can give the guests of the inn the feeling . . . that you do not know what you are doing. If you leave that feeling with the commercial man, he may be doubtful that he is receiving his calls from his customers; and, therefore, if this situation is prevailing, you could lose customers without ever knowing why."

An unhappy guest experience in one aspect of operations brings all aspects into suspicion. These were the kinds of truths we sensed we must find a way of communicating to managerial people in the new inns.

The moment I joined Kemmons Wilson and Wallace Johnson in the management of Holiday Inns, Inc., I was almost catapulted into this training challenge.

Barney McCool and Jack Ladd, rattling around the country in a beat-up station wagon, had already peddled a handful of $500 franchises to a half-dozen enterprising millionaires, with a cartload of promises but little actual back-up organization. Our legal department, for instance, was a front stall in an old plumbing shop that Wallace owned, where he and Kemmons and I huddled on packing crates to mastermind this latest business flyer of theirs. It didn't take long for the original franchisees to find out that the corporation was a single file drawer and one secretary, Wilma Roach, to handle correspondence!

Those astute investors were not about to set up an untested commercial venture in their home communities without a solid guarantee that they'd be given the know-how. They were sufficiently experienced with profit and loss realities to demand the safeguard of job-qualified personnel.

Staring me in the face from this franchise license contract was an assurance that the company (whatever *that* was!) would provide "30 days of training in Holiday Inn methods to a manager, a housekeeper, and a restaurant manager selected by Licensee . . ." Kemmons and Wallace themselves had several other irons in the fire besides this visionary motel chain, so they left it entirely to my devices to deliver on such a promise. They hadn't bothered to explain all those little details to me when they hired me, of course, because they intended for me to figure out for myself the job specifications for that impressive title they were giving me: executive vice-president.

It was their own attorney who warned them that they better let me put some meat on those naked franchise bones right soon. I went scurrying to every source of help I could find in order to begin drafting a manual of operations. I phoned to Atlanta and checked with the president of the Coca-Cola Company, who subsequently did me the great favor of sending the head of his legal department to Memphis to advise me. I even consulted the eminent Sam Stewart, president of the Bank of America out in San Francisco.

Some of my resources weren't quite so impressive. I dredged up every bit of personal business experience I'd ever had, going all the way back to adolescent days clerking in the Liberty Cash Grocery Store, where I'd had to learn to deal with distraught customers who had just had a fight with their husbands or wives and were taking out their wrath on anyone they saw.

That may have been the moment that I came upon Alfred P. Sloane's book, *My Years with General Motors,* which so inspired me that I determined, in my naiveté, to make the fledgling Holiday Inns, Inc., into the General Motors of the lodging industry.

I had one awesome strike against me. Those franchise holders I had to cope with were not men and women fresh out of school with stars in their eyes about some bright new horizon in the business world. To a person, they were seasoned and successful operators of their own enterprises— from finance to construction to dentistry to plumbing. They were buying a franchise and developing sources of major capital to open a pioneering establishment in their home communities that they fully expected would yield them a high return on their investment. They wanted the job done right, and no mistakes.

Between their rich and varied experience in business and my total lack of corporation experience (and of motel operations, most especially!), I began to lose a lot of sleep at nights.

I had no more taste for the assignment of convening them for an organizational meeting in Memphis than Daniel had for going into the lions' den! Some of those men were about ready to chew us to bits in the courts if necessary, and I didn't have what they were looking for.

What could I do? I had no choice. I called a first annual franchisees' convention for May 25, 1956, in a spare room Kemmons hadn't been able to rent in a new store building he owned. In that 25′ × 30′ space, the company officers and the licensees would square off, not more than thirty-five or forty of us, which was everybody involved with Holiday Inns at that point.

The night before, though, we entertained our guests at a reception and dinner. About nine o'clock, I suddenly remembered that I still didn't have a polished version of the constitution and by-laws ready for the next day's meeting, though I'd been working on it in bits and pieces for weeks.

By slaving on it through the night I was at last able, by four-thirty in the morning, to dictate the document in the form that they adopted the next day, and that was operational for years thereafter. So the promise of training had become official, and I had to design that thirty days' worth immediately.

Joe Vaterott, a major franchise holder who has been rightly known for years as "Mr. St. Louis," put his motion to approve in terms that made me feel both relieved and rewarded.

"Bill has done a fine job," he said, "and has captured the idea of what we're going to be doing."

Then and there, I learned the first secret in a successful training program: selling the vision.

You've got to excite the prospective trainees with a captivating picture of the business they are being enlisted to run. Even Jesus himself did that when he called the fishermen of Galilee to follow him so that he could make them fishers of men. It was something bigger than they had ever dreamed of, and they took off after him, and together they changed the history of the world.

Back in the midfifties, hotels and tourist homes and even motels were nothing new. What was the spark that would ignite the imaginations of these first Holiday Inns franchisees and motivate them to accept all our helpful training (yet to be developed!)?

Again, I thought about my ancestral namesake, Captain Walton of Carthage, Tennessee, and his inn on the toll road from Nashtown to Knoxtown in the late 1700s. It conjured up for me all I had ever heard and read about those early places of jovial hospitality and flowing good cheer in front of a huge open fireplace.

I had illustrious support on my side, too, in the words of the esteemed Dr. Samuel Johnson: "There is nothing which has yet been contrived by man by which so much happiness is produced as by a good inn."

I wasn't aware of any existing hotels like that in this country in our day, so I began to wax eloquent about Holiday Inns exhibiting "the fine old innkeeping tradition in a modern setting."

That got their attention. A little storytelling, a few word pictures, a touch of oratorical breathlessness in my voice— oh, the ham actor in me really rose to the occasion! They were all panting to plunge ahead into the new adventure by the time I got around to summarizing our philosophy in a more formal statement:

"We of Holiday Inns intend to bring to the traveling public of America the very finest in food and lodging, in an atmosphere of fireside human relationship, at a price reasonable for the traveling businessman and his family."

Training has got to start with an attractive target—some call it the organizational charter: What is the business aiming at? It's the way Lee Iacocca turned around the Chrysler Corporation, by emphasizing that their cars would be "the best . . . What else is there?" You simply cannot say too much for the value of a corporate vision in creating worker desire for training.

Consider a very simple example. In the lodging business, it doesn't take too much skill to teach a maid how to make up a bed, but WHY to do it a certain way is another matter. Why must the sheets be clean and smooth and pulled tight over the mattress and covered by a spread that hangs exactly the same distance from the floor on both sides of the bed?

Because we were serving guests at our inns, giving them just as much comfort and satisfaction and pleasure as if we were entertaining them in our homes. The maid was not just making a bed. She was making an impression. And the impression she made on guests through her workmanship spelled the difference between business being good or bad. And whether business was good or bad affected her income and job security.

It wasn't enough for that maid to walk away at the close of the day with relief that she'd gotten through the chore of readying thirteen rooms for their next occupants. We wanted her to leave with *pride* that "her" rooms would make the guests feel good so that they would want to stay at a Holiday Inn the next time they were traveling. The maid knew what we were about as a company. That helped her to accept instruction.

That's right, to accept. You have to motivate people for training just as much as for doing their job. Mediocre managers impose training requirements on employees. Excellent managers, by contrast, stimulate a team craving for help in doing a superior job to advance a business they all believe in. Once that spirit is generated, even the trainers are better motivated to develop a program that will measure up to expectations.

In the process of asking the crucial question of what their business is all about, some executives may come to the startling realization that what they are doing professionally doesn't really matter that much. That the enterprise they are putting their essential energy into is relatively meaningless. At that point, they can opt for cynicism or despair. Or they can seize the moment to create some fresh initiatives and incentives.

People in top management ought to be the ones who have the longest-range perspective on possibilities. They should not overlook any current difficulties, of course, but they should be able to see beyond them to new frontiers and new conquests. That's the Attitude of excellence that breeds corporate confidence, from officers right on through the ranks. When that's in place, everybody wants to get on with the job—and they are then ready to welcome the best training that management can make available to them.

At Holiday Inns, Inc., after describing a distinctive corporate vision and reason for being, we had to organize for achievement of that goal. Constitution and by-laws in place, the training had to begin in earnest.

New inns were popping up all over the place, and business and professional people, highly successful in their own fields, were practically standing in line to get into our burgeoning franchise system and to try their hand at being innkeepers. But they needed help.

Fortunately, we had the original four Wilson motels in Memphis through which we could illustrate and demonstrate the Holiday Inns distinctives. That's where we started, at 980 South Third Street in Memphis, with the indulgent cooperation of the neophyte innkeepers and their staff members, who were just beginning to learn their own jobs by doing them.

They were the people who helped me to put together the all-important operating manual, which I could picture only in terms of the Air Force manual, since there was nothing comparable to that in the hospitality industry as far as I'd been able to discover.

That volume stated right up front that our objective was to assure the public of "uniform, efficient, courteous, and high quality service on a standardized national basis." It dealt with everything from dripping faucets and mop stains on the baseboards to desk clerk telephone technique and an open Gideon Bible on the top of each bedside table. An example of it is this instruction about lobby temperature:

"Temperatures should be moderate and not geared to serve one or another person at the desk. The temperature has to be for the comfort of the public coming in and going out of the Inn and has to be kept moderate at all times."

We were particular about details for the simple reason that *everything* either reflected or affected our attitude toward the public. The manual ran to well over 200 pages, but it was not complicated or technical; it was just a basically common sense application of generally accepted hospitality standards, refined for our business setting.

At the time, it also had to be our primary training tool. To give some idea of the effort we put into making it practical, here is an excerpt from the section addressed to innkeepers:

> When you demonstrate how well you can teach, it builds confidence and respect. For example, if you are teaching how to clean a shower, say, "I like to clean the shower this way," and then go ahead and clean it, stressing the important points. Then have the employee clean a shower while you watch.
>
> This is the best type of instruction. It also assures that the job is being done right and impresses upon the employees that all jobs are important to the success of the inn.

Following that came a list of twenty teaching hints, divided among three headings: "Prepare Yourself as a Teacher," "Basic Steps in Training," "Innkeeper-Employee Relationship." We dealt with such simple things as listing the tasks, planning a schedule, selecting the right supplies and an appropriate setting. We gave suggestions on how to make the learner feel at ease, spark learner interest, present material in a variety of ways, stress what was of major importance, and limit each session to reach a realistic teaching objective. There was provision for both try-out sessions and feedback opportunities for the learner.

Naturally, we went beyond mechanical functions associated with the job, since we always had the aim of instilling the Attitude. So we underscored the sense of belonging to the corporate family, identified incentives and rewards, explained disciplinary measures, outlined the organizational structure and policies, and—our motivational ace at all times—we told the Holiday Inns story!

You can see even from that brief summary that we didn't take anything for granted. But because the Attitude of respect for individuals was absolutely intrinsic to the Holiday Inns idea, we took the innkeepers through a few more pages of specifics that applied to them. As I look back over my original version of the manual now, I think we managed to hit on timeless principles that are as valid today as when we started. What has changed, for instance, in basic pointers on "How to Get Along with Others"? We got right down to cases on topics like gossiping, grouchiness, undue familiarity, untidiness, boisterousness, tardiness, bad manners, and poor taste.

As I told our people so often, the competition might be able to match anything else we could do by way of inn construction and features and rates, but they'd have to go some to catch up with the high standards reflected in the attitude of our work force. I wish the same emphasis characterized employee dress and deportment in far more of the businesses and offices I find myself having to visit these days.

My point is that excellence in training must tend to particulars. In the operational manual, the material on training included another section that laid the motivational basis for much of what preceded it in the regulations I've just described. We headed it "Working for Others." At Holiday Inns, we worked for the public, and the whole hierarchy of company jobs was designed and defined as ultimately serving the public's best interests.

If that has a faintly familiar ring to it, it ought to; it's what's been known for two millennia as the Golden Rule.

Each business, of course, has to develop the peculiar

specifications of its own training program. The one challenge they all face in common, however, is how to motivate
employee enrollment—other than through coercion. One of
the ways we tried to úse a little friendly persuasion was to
demonstrate, harmlessly I hope, the potentially disastrous
consequences of no training.

At our annual franchisees' meeting one year, for example, we confronted the group with some recorded examples
of front desk responses to telephone calls. Over the public
address system in the auditorium boomed the voices of an
anonymous caller and a variety of equally anonymous desk
clerks. The object was to illustrate how many times the
phone had to ring before anyone answered it, and then what
kind of etiquette was used.

The franchise-holders alternately groaned or roared with
laughter as they heard two-way conversations that revealed
all kinds of inept and even inconsiderate employee handling
of inquiries. When this sequence ended, we disclosed to the
audience that all the calls they heard had been placed by a
company representative posing as a potential guest. They
were more than ready to concede the need for continued
employee training.

Another motivational encouragement for training is to
upgrade employee perception of the role they are being
trained for. I loved to do this with incoming groups of innkeepers, since the prospects before them really were terrific
beyond their realizing.

"You must recognize today that you are operating a mil-
lion-dollar business in even the smallest Holiday Inn," I told
them. "You must be good in marketing, personnel administration, industrial relations, inventory control, pricing of
your products, advertising, public affairs, and all other basic
elements of sound business administration."

That catalog was enough to make anybody want help,

no matter how good a business background they brought with them into the system. But I had a further challenge for them.

"More than anything else," I continued, "you are a leader. You are the one individual in that Holiday Inn whom all of the people look to for guidance and for motivation. You must lead by example, not by dictate. You cannot sit behind your desk and write your memorandums and send out edicts, and think by that to manage that Holiday Inn."

What they heard me say in that speech was reinforced by what I had written into the operating manual in the special section for innkeepers. There, too, I tried to impress on them the importance of their role—that they must never be self-satisfied just because their inn was run efficiently, but that they must always keep up with new developments in serving travelers.

In other words, I tried to challenge the innkeepers with an incentive to keep learning. Several pages followed, detailing how to build success as an innkeeper, outlining daily and weekly duties, and addressing matters such as writing business letters, analyzing advertising methods, and even affiliating with the local Chamber of Commerce and other organizations.

I bore down on principles of interpersonal relationships with staff: setting an example, counseling, motivating to reach full potential, explaining why as well as telling what when necessary, providing the best tools, and the right working conditions.

Pondering a list that was much more extensive than that, even a seasoned innkeeper would get a renewed sense of the multifaceted task that extended beyond merely running the business and keeping records. One explanation why executives sometimes fail to motivate employees to seek training is their failure to communicate the magnitude of the responsibility.

There's still another very effective method of instilling a desire to receive assistance from company training programs: regular inspections. Each inn was visited at least four times annually by a corps of company inspectors, with a follow-up report to the innkeeper—and to the owner—on any deficiencies noted on the exhaustive checksheet. Failure to bring operations into compliance resulted in penalties ranging all the way up to license cancellation. At the same time, inns appearing in the top 10 percent of inspection ratings were awarded a certificate of merit, and the best inn received an award of $1,000.

The theme of annual conferences reinforced the urgency of maintaining the integrity of the system by meeting all standards. Regional workshops throughout the year guided innkeepers and restaurant managers in service improvements and stimulated their motivation by providing an opportunity to exchange ideas and explore solutions to common operational problems.

By such means, local managers did not feel isolated or insulated, and they were eager to measure up by taking advantage of company help.

The pressure on us to improve training procedures increased with the unexpected rate of our business expansion. Even in the first couple of years, the rising number of inns open and operating multiplied the work force dramatically. It soon became obvious that we would have to do training in the field as well as at home base. From then on, we focused on management personnel training in Memphis through what we called the Holiday Inns Training School, and did staff training in the field, with headquarters teams visiting all inns periodically.

So firmly committed was I to the indispensability of thorough and ongoing employee training for everyone from innkeeper to busboy, that I began to promote my private dream of someday building a Holiday Inn University for that singular purpose.

There I was, with a high school education and a night school law degree, fantasizing that I could blaze a trail and set a standard for the entire industry!

Was that an ego trip? I'm sure there must have been a lot of that involved. After all, I was the tail end of the founding team—Wilson, the innovator, and Johnson were partners in a way that I was not. Their dream already had materialized before I was invited to contribute to it through my legal skills and administrative abilities. Sure, it would be very gratifying to me to start something of my own within the company.

But, having admitted all of that, I think I can say honestly that I was far more driven by my enthusiasm for making Holiday Inns not only the biggest but the best in the business. I wanted the people who worked in our company to feel that we regarded them as deserving of the best that money could buy and that technology could produce. We were the acknowledged leader in the industry, and we were willing to give the Holiday Inns family every advantage for maintaining that position. Nothing less than first class would do for our people.

The concept of a training center with state-of-the-art facilities represented a vote of confidence in the company of hard-working employees dedicated to the Attitude we worked so hard to instill in them. To perpetuate and extend the motivation and skills to future generations of employees would reaffirm the founding ideals and help to keep us great.

Any company that wants to preserve and promote what it stands for cannot leave the job to the public relations department. An external image readily slips out of sync with internal actualities if company management is not perennially keeping its people imbued with the chartered vision and up-grading their ability to fulfill it.

From the time I first ventured to expose the idea of a Holiday Inn University, we had lively discussion about it in board meetings. Executives know what I mean by "lively discussion"! There was plenty of resistance to such a costly project, but my stubborn streak was a yard wide by then, and I stuck to my campaign.

One day in the boardroom, after another crusading charge by me, from an unexpected source (Wallace, in fact) came the half-exasperated comment: "Kemmons, why don't you just let Bill go ahead and build his school?"

The chairman of the board sat there quietly for a moment, while I was trying to recover from my surprise at this endorsement. Then he reached into his pocket and pulled out his white handkerchief. He deliberately unfolded it, and then raising it above his head, he waved it aloft in a silent gesture of surrender!

As if that weren't enough, he flabbergasted me by pledging the first $250,000 to launch the project. His partner, Wallace, who was by then the vice-chairman of the board, followed his good example with a matching pledge.

Although he had opposed it strenuously for a long time, Kemmons would later go on record as saying, "The Holiday Inn University will be part of the continuing education in skills and attitude which we feel is so vital to our success."

The $4 million Holiday Inn University was dedicated on October 23, 1972. Situated on its own eighty-eight rolling acres in Olive Branch, Mississippi, just about twelve miles south of corporate headquarters in Memphis, it duplicated a first-class Holiday Inn lodging (184 rooms and eight suites—our "dormitory") and 260-seat restaurant structure, plus the finest conference capabilities for handling 5,000 persons each year in its programs. There's also a small lake modeled after the one I designed for my own estate, a swimming pool, a golf course, and an adjacent airstrip that can accommodate corporate jet planes.

There's no reason, as I see it, why employee training can't take place in attractive and enjoyable surroundings. In fact, *where* the training is offered can do fully as much for motivation and results as *what* training is offered. Again, it's that underlying company Attitude of respect for individuals and caring for their needs.

Besides being an expanded Holiday Inn where the instruction can be given in a setting identical to the future work situation, the university contained "laboratories" for testing innkeeping and food and beverage innovations. The main classroom is an amphitheater equipped for a full range of audiovisual presentations.

Unlike most other schools, every residence room at the university became a learning center through two closed circuit television channels used daily to provide review and preparatory material, allowing self-paced and repetitive study by the individual trainee. Instructional videotapes, produced in the university's own television studio facilities when we first began, could be relayed to 240 different locations in the complex.

Since the university was fully staffed in every department with the same personnel that any inn would have, as many as 160 employees, trainees in residence had daily opportunity to observe all inn procedures, from housekeeping and food service to accounting and yard maintenance.

The programs we instituted were designed to train inn-keepers, restaurant managers, housekeepers, hostesses, maintenance supervisors, sales representatives, marketing people, and others with managerial assignments. The intention was that each person enrolled in such management-oriented courses would assume a major training responsibility for their own employees at each local inn.

The on-the-job skill training for local employees continued to be enhanced by a field staff that moved constantly from place to place for short-term instruction and by audiovisual materials circulated throughout the system for on-site use.

Leadership techniques, then, were a major component in the university's educational concept. A new innkeeper usually brings to the job considerable previous experience and education. But it was never assumed that the original four-week orientation term at the university and the checklists in the operating manual were sufficient to fulfill the training necessary. All innkeepers were required to return annually for continuing education seminars of shorter duration. Every good training program must incorporate regular retraining.

What the university experience was intended to give its students were the tools to become better managers and supervisors. It provided a framework within which they had opportunity for continued development and for reevaluation of their own skills and attitudes. The ultimate aim, as in every sound educational process, is self-understanding and self-realization, blended with the philosophies and goals of the business context in which they work. Thus prepared, they can undertake the training of all employees under their supervision.

An important by-product was that the university could

serve as a communication hub for the entire system. Through resident classes, the field training staff, and required yearly continuing education seminars, vital information could be constantly updated and transmitted to all management personnel. New operational developments and new techniques could be put into practice with relative ease. Marketing programs could be discussed between planners and managers, assuring better understanding and cooperation.

Above all, as I saw it, the university would provide the best channel for refreshing throughout the Holiday Inn family that motivational Attitude we considered the secret of our corporate success. The motto said it all: "SERVARE— To Serve." The certificates we issued periodically to mark successful completion of study phases each carried a code letter that, after a thousand course hours of study, combined to spell out the word *PRIDE*, an acrostic embodying our key commitments: Perseverance, Responsibility, Integrity, Discipline, Enthusiasm.

Worldwide expansion of Holiday Inns made necessary a multilingual approach to training. Many of our people needed to know a second or even a third language in their place of work. As overseas franchisees sent personnel to study at the university, we had to offer multilingual instructional materials. At one point, we had a manager who knew eleven languages! In today's business world, there's practically a premium on such abilities, even in the American domestic scene.

A special aspect of the university program was what we called executive development. This continuing education emphasis sought to develop employees who were prospects for corporate advancement, and it became almost a hallmark of Holiday Inns management concepts. Instruction covered a wide range of subjects from telephone techniques and business letter writing to oral communicative skills for those required to speak before groups or make oral presentations and reports.

In order to assure our people that the training they were receiving was not ingrown, limited to our own corporate experience and perceptions, I encouraged the use of visiting faculty from time to time, especially in the summer. We were pleased to have distinguished professors from Harvard University's School of Business Administration, for example, come to share their insights with our students. And the interaction among the students themselves, coming as they did from diverse cultural backgrounds around the world, was always richly educational in itself.

Even before the university came into existence, I was concerned to provide opportunity for promising young company personnel to be acquainted with broader points of view in the management field than simply our own party line.

We developed Operation Dynamo, a cooperative program with the School of Business Administration at Memphis State University, that included over seventy hours of special instruction in accounting, commercial law, marketing, sales, written and oral communications, economics, business organization, insurance, and other pertinent subjects. Anyone who desired could attend night sessions to improve their abilities and their chances for advancement. The two-year program graduated eighty in a short while, including at least eight executives who received officerships or promotions based partly on their participation.

As corporate officers, we knew that we were doing some things right because the evidence was substantial. But, at the same time, we knew that we had to keep on learning as we went along and to keep updated in our field. The attention to continuing education of junior executives and middle management was one way that we at the top ourselves could stay abreast of developments.

Training should always be perceived by workers as an opportunity not as an obligation. It should be considered one of the employee benefits, in the finest sense of that word. Workers in a business should vie with each other for a chance to take all of it that they can get.

We never had any trouble persuading people in our company-owned inns or in the franchise operations to travel to rural Mississippi for some intensive instruction at the university.

I have taken all this time to detail the Holiday Inn University story in order to emphasize that to take training seriously as a management responsibility demands the ultimate in imagination, initiative, and investment. The best product or the finest service in the world will never be able to make the grade if the people who manufacture it or who render it to the public are ignorant or inept.

Training costs a lot.

It pays even more.

In a statement prepared for the 1970 franchisees' conference, Kemmons observed, "While specific education and training is unidentifiable in the lower right hand corner of the operating statement reflecting profits, I feel that it will very definitely play a part in increasing profits . . ." That perception undoubtedly helped him to come around in support of the university idea.

In 1973 a prestigious honor came our way when *Institutions* magazine selected Holiday Inns, Inc., to receive its annual Changemaker Award. Previous winners had included the Marriott Corporation, Club Mediterranee, and Walt Disney Productions.

In her letter to Kemmons on April 3, officially notifying him that we were the 1973 choice, editor-in-chief Jane Y. Wallace wrote:

> Our criteria for choosing a Changemaker include innovation, imagination, pioneering management techniques—and just plain success.
>
> The 1973 Changemaker Award is presented to Holiday Inns for developing outstanding training methods and especially for success in building a "second generation" team of dedicated young people.

That tribute probably capped my tenure as president; but more than that, it validated my contention that training must be given a company's wholehearted backing if it was to achieve distinction and serve the best interests of the business.

I never missed a chance at the university to welcome incoming groups of trainees or to address each graduating class in person. The capable director of the university could have done a good job of it, of course. But, again with that desire to touch our people with care, I wanted those employees to know that the president of Holiday Inns, Inc., rated their attendance and their efforts to help us do a better job for the public, as worthy of his own highest priority.

I told every group—whether innkeepers or housekeepers, sales representatives or heads of subsidiaries—that the quality of their work was the real secret of their company's phenomenal growth and influence in the industry. I told them that we in the home office believed in our heavy investment in their training because, to the traveling public, those inn employees were finally what Holiday Inns were all about.

Motivational pep talks? Sure, why not? It never hurt a company's profits, as far as I know, for workers to feel confident that their best efforts mattered to the boss.

It's so easy for executives to accept figurehead status in the corporate structure as far as the bulk of their employees is concerned. They dwell on that Olympian summit of tycoonery, shrouded in the mists and mysteries (and myths) of top management, seldom glimpsed and almost never heard by the company people.

But if ever there were a place where the boss has more at stake and should take a hands-on interest and would be most welcome to make a personal appearance, it's where the troops gather for marching orders. It's one thing for executive management to provide training—which should be the very best that can be devised. Excellence in this regard, however, as everywhere else, calls also for executive involvement. Even if it's only poking your head into the classroom long enough to say, "Glad you're all here . . . You're doing a fine job . . . Carry on . . . We're depending on you!"

Provide for employee training with a caring touch, and the working ranks will reach back with enthusiastic support for corporate goals and objectives.

# 5. Using Competition
## Can the People Improve the Job?

It's only short-sighted executives who think they don't need rank-and-file support, considering the competition every business faces. Perhaps nothing underscores more dramatically a company's need for a well-trained work force than the ogre of competition. If your people don't know how to do their jobs, your business doesn't stand a chance of surviving in the overcrowded marketplace.

Some of the competition comes from inside, just in the natural course of doing what you're supposed to be doing. At Holiday Inns headquarters we had to handle a sizable number of complaints each year! As Wallace Johnson observed with his wry wit: "Each night we have nearly 250,000 people staying with us, so we can make more people mad in a twenty-four-hour span than anyone else I know!"

One of our guests ingeniously registered his complaint against us. It seems that he had stopped in a number of our restaurants trying to get a taste of the juicy steak we advertised. He sent us a copy of the ad, with this cryptic but eloquent note:

"Sir, you've got to be kidding."

It's imperative to keep up the company standards. One of the ironies we have to deal with in merchandising our goods and services is that, as a result of affluence, customer dissatisfaction increases rather than decreases. The economic ability to make choices brings with it more differentiation and discernment. When customers can make many price and value comparisons, confusion easily results and wise selection becomes difficult.

The greatest challenge to a business in a situation like this is how to make it easier for the public to consistently choose what it is offering.

At the 1968 annual conference, I reported that we had received 1,753 complaints about reservations so far that year.

"That's like the tip of the iceberg," I told the franchisees. "About 90% is below the surface. Many customers don't bother to complain. They just get mad and go somewhere else to stay."

That same year's statistics also revealed 1,122 complaints about rooms, 663 about billings and refunds, and 874 about service. Add them up and it all sounds rather ominous. I can't resist telling you, though, that those 1,753 reservations complaints were against year-to-date total registrations at Holiday Inns of 18,500,000! The iceberg of unhappy people could not have been *too* large.

We commissioned the Gallup organization to do a public survey for us to see how well we stacked up against the competition. The results made us feel pretty good. The number who had heard of us was 96%, in contrast to 92% for the next best-known motel system. That gave us some documentation for thinking that we had become a household name in our first sixteen years. Also, 65% had actually stayed for a night or more at a Holiday Inn, as opposed to 43% for the next most popular.

As to rating factors in order of importance: 77% put having reservations in order at the top or near it; 69% thought "friendly, helpful employees" came next, followed by 67% voting for "pleasant dining atmosphere," and 62% each for "cordial reception" and "fast restaurant service."

(It's worth noting how many of those factors can be directly influenced through employee training procedures.)

So despite some internal shortcomings that marred the record, it boiled down to our being reassured that we were still responding well to the needs and desires of the traveling public, both commercial people and families.

Therein lay a great danger for us, though. The adage "Nothing succeeds like success" has some merit to it, but can be very misleading. One thing I've had sadly impressed on me is that "Nothing *seduces* like success"!

How many good and prosperous companies have fallen on hard times for no other reason than complacency? They received a good public reaction to begin with, built up revenues over the years by providing an acceptable product or service, and then suddenly seemed to fall by the wayside.

Various temptations come to a company when things are going well, but I think complacency is one of the most devastating. It's as if management says, "We've got it made. Let's just relax."

Lots of businesses lose their soul in success. They began by caring for the people they were serving and then drifted into a casual attitude that quickly degenerated into contempt. They stopped trying to please, without seeming to take into account that times and tastes change. Employees and public alike were the losers.

People in top management may be the most vulnerable of all to that flawed thnking. It is not deliberate but probably arises from some built-in glitch in the enterprise itself. When a business starts small, the executive leadership, sometimes just a single person, enjoys running things on a daily basis. The work force is minimal and the customers relatively few, so the boss can easily keep check on everything.

With growth of business volume, enlargement of payroll, and proliferation of company activities, administrative responsibility has to be divided and spread. But the old mentality remains that personal oversight, with final decision-making authority, is the right way to maintain the original thrust.

If you're dealing with a Mom-and-Pop operation, you can get by with that thinking. But when you become a national and multinational corporation, it's executive insanity to think that one person can head the business with all the former attentiveness and wisdom.

In the rapid expansion of Holiday Inns, I did a lot as executive vice-president to bolster that myth by promoting the Wilson entrepreneurship as symbolic of what the company was all about. He was the outraged father of five who returned from a vacation trip to start a better highway lodging system for families. It made a terrific human interest story, and the traveling public could identify with it completely.

The problem was that Kemmons couldn't conduct company affairs the same way in 1975 as in 1955, for the simple reason that by then, in the combined parent company inns and the franchise group, we had 150,000 people working for us in more than fifty countries, not only managing inns but also operating vast divisions and diverse subsidiaries. He needed to learn that he could no longer oversee every aspect of company business. Just because certain methods had worked in the beginning did not mean that twenty years later they would still work.

Complacency can tempt all of us to think that tried and true administrative methods never need revising. In whatever form it takes, it is a bad business attitude for the simple reason that it takes people for granted. It's a case of thinking the wrong way about people, and it breeds mediocrity.

You've almost got to keep nagging at your employees about excellence if you're going to save them from slipping into complacency. But managers need to take periodic inventory of themselves, too, to see if they are performing as good as their word where the company people are concerned.

How contempt for the public can creep in through complacency and self-satisfaction, almost unnoticed, is sadly easy to illustrate. One year at the annual conference, I had to bear down on an undesirable peak-season practice of some of our inn owners, which I called "selective selling." Under this policy, an innkeeper would turn away a single person seeking a room, or charge that person the full double rate, simply because all that was left was a double room. Unsatisfied with the average proportion of single and double occupancy, those operators tried to have a full house of double occupancies.

More revenue was their goal, of course, and I couldn't blame them for that. But it was a woefully short-sighted practice. That single who was turned away might have stayed at that inn ten times more during that year. He or she may have spent more in the restaurant and lounge than most families and recommended the inn to more people. I told the franchisees and their innkeepers in no uncertain terms that I did not view selective selling as best service but as worst service. Furthermore, that practice was competing with themselves and cutting their own throats in the process.

We had a great bunch of men and women in our Holiday Inns system, but they were vulnerable like everyone else to the "master passion Gain," as Dickens put it. I said to them on one occasion:

"A Holiday Inn owner is a capitalist. Some capitalists are of the 'Get mine and get out' school. Buy a property, make all the money you can, then sell it. They're not the kind who own Holiday Inns."

With somewhat loftier rhetoric, I told them, "The pages of history reflect the written truth of humankind from the beginning of time, which cannot be denied, and cries out: Beware of greed, for it is the root of the tree of self-destruction."

Such scoldings from the boss have their place sometimes, but there's a much more effective way of dealing with complacency. I almost hesitate to mention it, because it can so easily get out of control and have destructive results. If carefully managed, however, interdepartmental competition at the management level can really keep the corporate juices flowing. It makes the competitive spirit work for the company's best interests rather than against them.

Very early in our history, I introduced some challenges between division heads, department heads, and even some of the subsidiary heads. In the Lake House at Glen Echo, my home in the country, I'd convene an annual planning meeting for the company's profit-center and department directors. In preparation, each of them spent many days readying their respective presentations of the bottom-line profit their division would contribute to the company in the coming year.

The biggest competitive situation was between franchise sales and innkeepers supply. Sessions could get very hot as the participants listened to each other and then raised their challenges.

"You should be ashamed of yourself," Clyde Dixon might say to Jeff Mann. "You know you can sell more franchises than that!"

Mann would retort, "I do all of your selling for you. I

sell the franchise, and then you tell the franchise holder that he must buy his furnishings and equipment from you!"

Sometimes several of them would join ranks and gang up on one person in particular: "Your contribution to the profit picture of Holiday Inns is a disgrace."

There were times when I wasn't so much chairman of the meeting as referee. But at the end of two or three days, we'd hammer out our forecasts and our goals for the new year. It could be a grueling experience, hibernating as we did for such an extended period of time, having our meals catered from the university or the Poplar Avenue Holiday Inn. But I had the impression they all looked forward to this annual donnybrook, finding it stimulating to their determination to do a job they could be proud of among their peers.

Quarterly, I'd get the same group together to review progress toward the annual goal. In between times, the various heads would also meet with the executive committee to make their reports and take their bows—or sometimes a kick in the pants!

Complacency doesn't have as good a chance when managers know they're scheduled periodically to hear either "Well done . . . Congratulations!" or "What happened?"

The profit centers and departments weren't the only ones who had their feet held to the fire, though. We on the executive staff were scrutinized, too, as to our effectiveness in cost control. Sometimes we had to answer rather embarrassing questions. Kemmons and I were quizzed on how we could justify riding around in the Learjet, often alone. Even though he was company founder and chief executive officer, Kemmons was challenged now and then about certain corporate acquisitions.

The dreamers among us, who had ambitious plans for developments in their areas, had to go through tedious and tense justifications over and over again before they could hope to win the chance to try. The rewards for persistence and striving for achievement came to many of our people with the publishing of the annual report and the holding of the stockholders' meeting, when each head and team would get recognition for goals met.

Internal competition, when it's kept on a friendly and wholesome basis, packs terrific motivational punch to counteract a lackadaisical attitude or contentment with the status quo.

Management must keep a watchful eye, though, that internal competition *is* friendly. I'd be kidding you if I gave the impression that we didn't have some vigorous—I'll even admit to vicious—rivalries within the ranks. The one immorality I despised above all others whenever and however it showed up was back stabbing.

There was a period of time in the early seventies when all kinds of forces were at work in the world at large and in the business community in particular that should have motivated workers in our company and every other to band together in the most enlightened self-interest. Instead a few opportunists took advantage of the unrest to advance their private agendas. It happened at Holiday Inns, Inc., like many other places. I felt the knife between my own ribs, and the scars from it last a long time.

The problem is that all the family image promoted among the rank-and-file workers was contradicted at the top executive level. We could hardly expect employees to embrace each other with respect and affection when we upstairs were engaging in mortal combat.

Executives can forget all about excellence if they permit

the competitive spirit to get out of hand anywhere within the company, especially at the top where it's most visible to everybody.

It's one thing to urge your people to take more training for improving their work. It's another to convey the impression that you're training them for a war of self-advancement. Excellence is the Attitude of respect for the dignity of the individual. It can't coexist with contemptuous competition within the ranks.

Another sly seduction of success is underestimating the external competition. When you introduce something new into the marketplace, you can expect imitators to spring up overnight. A lot of the time, what they offer the public is bogus, a cheap copy of the real thing, and their enterprise is short-lived.

But other responsible companies also see what you have done, recognize it as a good thing that's here to stay, and promptly latch onto it themselves with a few improvements and refinements to give them their market share. In fact, if others don't do their thing differently because you did your thing better first, you are not truly   leader!

All of that is part of the strengt ı of the free enterprise system. Anybody is welcome to take a crack at beating out the opposition with a better product. I welcome that kind of incentive because it keeps everybody on their toes.

At Holiday Inns, a lot of the innovations that we introduced into the lodging industry were adopted or adapted soon by others and became standard. What they did wasn't always better than what we did, but sometimes it looked nicer and might even cost less.

They could build a bigger swimming pool, for instance, or use fancier room decorating. We had to take such challenges seriously, but at the same time we were so far ahead of everybody else in number of inns and volume of service that we never did run scared of the competition.

Not for the first twenty years, at least. But that picture changed, too. Sometimes it has almost nothing to do with competitors in your own field of business, but with other kinds of opposition. Government regulatory agencies, for one example. On the one hand, they can keep a business on its toes, seeing that it honors agreements and fulfills promises. On the other hand, they can sometimes be so overbearing in their requirements that business initiative is stifled by excessive paperwork.

The policies of foreign governments can also squeeze business in this country. The oil embargo of 1973–74, for instance, severely damaged the tourist industry. One response of our government was to order weekend closing of gasoline stations. In just four months, that decision cost travel-related enterprises in this country nearly three-quarters of a *billion* dollars! It put 90,000 people out of work and jeopardized the jobs of another 179,000. (Incidentally, that drastic action saved very little gasoline.)

It put Holiday Inns into an unaccustomed and desperate scramble with all the other industry leaders to muster a market share for ourselves. According to an article about Holiday Inns in *Business Week* for September 7, 1974, company stock that had reached a high of 55+ in 1972 was then at 10+. That's a brand of competition that's hard to combat.

Yet even in tough economic times you can use ingenuity to capitalize on the liability. You can use the occasion to rally your people to do a better job than ever so that others in your line of business will be outclassed by your quality of service. Training under those tougher circumstances may be more sought after by employees than in easier times, because their spirit of loyalty to the company rises to meet the heightened challenge. Again, make the competition work for you.

While internal complacency and varieties of external competition are perils that go along with success, there is one temptation more devastating than all the rest, in my opinion. And that one hit us hard at Holiday Inns, almost causing our undoing and eventually altering the very character of the company.

That temptation, or seduction, is expansion.

Nobody in the business world is going to criticize expansion. After all, that's practically the name of the game. Growth, whether in a private business or in the nation's gross national product, seems to be the summum bonum to which we all aspire. Growth and progress are related, and there is no resting place for an enterprise in a competitive economy. In that regard, when growth stops, decline begins.

Kemmons's original dream was for a string of 400 Holiday Inns flashing their star from coast to coast. That wasn't a magic number, particularly, except that it was large in comparison with the four motels in Memphis. It was an arbitrary number, picked to represent the dream of providing highway travelers with the Holiday Inn home-away-from-home atmosphere at the end of every day's drive, even when that was cross-continental. He had service in mind, not growth for its own sake.

In fact, even in retirement Kemmons still gets most of his fun out of life by starting new enterprises. He likes successful growth statistics as well as the next fellow, but it's making things happen that really turns him on. He's still at it.

At the University of Alabama in Birmingham in 1971, Kemmons told the students, "I don't know anything more thrilling than to see an idea develop into a profitable enterprise. Maybe it's a creative thing. Some people write poetry or paint pictures. I build businesses."

The historic fact of the matter, of course, is that Holiday Inns was a runaway success, with our 1,000th inn opening only thirteen years after we organized. We grew almost without trying because we were bringing to the market something the people of America—and of the world, as it turned out—had a pent-up postwar appetite for. The time was ripe for our "old-fashioned innkeeping tradition in a modern setting."

That kind of growth pace necessitates certain kinds of expansion in any business. For us, the sheer volume of our need for building materials, furnishings, food, and other supplies made it smart for us to develop our own company subsidiaries to be our suppliers. In some cases we bought up existing businesses who were servicing us, or we developed entirely new resources under our own auspices.

Innkeepers Supply Company, for instance, grew initially as one of our divisions to take care of our Holiday Inns needs until it was actually servicing many of our competitors throughout the industry as well. Volume meant high efficiency and lower prices, so we were performing a service for everyone in the food and lodging business who wanted to take advantage of it.

All of this spells expansion with a capital "E." Naturally, it means tremendous personnel expansion as well, as departments multiply and divisions have to be created to group them compatibly. And you have got to make doubly sure that you surround yourself with people who really know what they are doing.

The training imperative is never more crucial than when a business is experiencing rapid growth. Long gone were the days when the three of us—Kemmons, Wallace, and I—sat around on packing crates and figured out the budget together on a yellow legal pad!

But in the business paradise such as we were enjoying, the wily serpent, as always, insinuates a sly suggestion: "Since you're relishing all of this so much, why not try something even better that's bound to increase your pleasure?"

We were already stretching our luck by getting into all those supply subsidiaries who produced things that we knew nothing directly about, except as we were the consumer for them in Holiday Inns operations. But now the alluring fruit hanging on the transportation tree in the garden of tourism was what we called "Tco," a combine of Continental Trailways Bus Company and Delta Steamship Lines as chief components.

We Holiday Inns executives, romping ecstatically around our paradise, weren't satisfied with all the goodies we'd savored up until then. This looked delicious to some among us: a linkage between the leader of the lodging industry and a giant in transportation. The buses and the steamships were simply other vehicles besides automobiles to bring the traveling public to our hospitable doors. What a reasonable union of business interests it seemed.

What a seduction it turned out to be.

I wish I could say that I stopped that acquisition. Instead, I voted for it. It was not an action I took in faith, because the prospects actually gave me a lot of uneasiness. I vigorously expressed some of my misgivings in board discussions and in the executive committee meetings, but it didn't seem like a place where I should take my last stand and fight, so I reluctantly went along with it.

We bought trouble.

Today, mergers, acquisitions, and takeovers have become so commonplace that our story may seem archaic. But our experience could well have been a lesson to a lot of more recent business conglomerates that should have thought twice before doing what they did.

We knew our business very well, the hospitality business, and we were making an enviably good record at it. We didn't know one thing about buses and boats. But we sure found out a lot in a hurry, and none of it was good. The fruit that had tantalized the corporate eye turned bitter on the corporate tongue.

There's little point now in recounting the capital expenses, union conflicts (the only ones in Holiday Inns history up to that point), the revenue drains, and the other disadvantages that accrued to us during the years associated with this merger.

It might be worth noting, however, that when the big shuffle of top management occurred at Holiday Inns in the late seventies, one of the announced objectives of the new leadership was divestiture of burdensome subsidiary enterprises and a return to concentration on the hospitality business. Within five or six years, that reversal of conglomeration was completed, and continuing expansion of the company settled on hospitality-related enterprises as the present management interprets them.

Success breeds the delusion that because you can do one thing well, you can do all things equally well. The temptation comes to think you can beat the competition by swallowing it. That simply isn't true.

Obviously, it wouldn't hurt to have periodic training courses for top management, too, just to keep them reminded of what they keep telling their employees concerning the purposes of the corporation and the skills needed to achieve them! Good training keeps priorities straight.

Tendencies toward complacency and self-satisfaction, internal rivalries and grievances, and unbridled expansionism are potentially negative elements that should prompt management to reinforce the company training program as a safeguard of values that need to be reaffirmed. The threats are bound to crop up and cannot be treated lightly, but neither should they be feared.

Another one of Wallace's famous aphorisms went something like this: "If you find yourself stuck with a lemon, make lemonade!"

He's probably right. Turn competition, internal and external, into momentum to create improved training for better performance—and have the last laugh on your opponents!

# 6. Stimulating Initiative
## Can the People Grow on the Job?

Is it possible that even the best-motivated and best-run training program can get out of hand and give the executives of a company something unexpected to cope with? I mean simply this:

Train another person well enough, and you might find your *own* job in jeopardy!

Incentive for employees to accept or seek training depends strongly on where it leads. Most workers rightly assume that job improvement merits job advancement. They want to get ahead, not just get better at what they're already doing. When they have gone through the company training program, they naturally want a chance to show what they can do with their new skills, to take on new challenges, and to compete for promotion.

That can become a threat to executive encouragement of initiative. The highest rungs on the corporate ladder are the shakiest. To feel some energetic young climber impatiently shoving from below can precipitate a premature step from the top to—Where? In sheer self-defense, therefore, managers may stifle initiative in their junior associates.

I'm fairly sensitive on the subject. I was ony thirty-four years old when I started off at Holiday Inns, Inc., as number three from the top and was further honored with the designation "Cofounder." There was so much excitement in running the daily operations of a business miracle for those first fifteen years or so that I didn't give much thought to eventually stepping up. Oh, now and then, I confess, working so close to the pioneering partners Kemmons and Wallace, who both were a number of years older than myself, I figured to stand on the top rung someday.

In the course of time, I did move up: from executive vice-president, to president, to vice-chairman of the board. My foot was practically poised in midair for the last half-step when suddenly . . . no more climbing room!

Kemmons and Wallace were gone, but "Chairman of the Board" was painted on someone else's door, not mine. I was hurt, angry, bitter.

By then, of course, the Holiday Inns executive roster was loaded with group presidents, senior vice-presidents, and vice-presidents ad infinitum. And a lot of those up-and-coming younger company leaders were my protégés, people that I had grilled and groomed and granted a place to hang their shingles. I was proud of them, and I had told more than one of them that anytime they thought they were mature enough to do it, they could make their move to take my job.

I think I'm qualified to talk about both the dark and the bright sides of building initiative through training. When my father left home for good, in his remorse over depression business failures that were really beyond his control, my socialite mother had to find a paying job for the first time in her life. I was twelve, and I went to work, too, to help support my younger sister and brother and the precious grandmother who lived with us. Such initiative was not my free choice, but the necessity in our family circumstances released an inner force that I can still feel driving me to this day. It's still in my soul to want to show what I can do.

That boyhood recollection makes me think of another dimension of promoting initiative that's often overlooked by employers but has long-term impact: recruitment of future personnel among the families of employees.

It's fine to bring people up the ladder within company ranks, but what about the replacements and reinforcements that have to be added? Personnel departments are always on the lookout for qualified and promising new people. But I wonder if many of them don't overlook an obvious source right on their doorstep. If you operate a company that is people-centered, and if you take into account the impact that the Attitude can have indirectly in the homes of employees and among their circles of friends, let recruitment begin there.

In the summer of 1974, we held our first of several second-generation happenings at the university. It gave the older sons and daughters of employees and franchisees, and other friends an inside look at the food and lodging industry. We thought it was an ideal way to stimulate career goals, and we didn't hesitate to suggest that the young people follow their parents into the Holiday Inn company or system.

If a father and mother talk about their work enthusiastically when they get home at night, how much more informative and influential might be the direct observation of what goes on at the work location?

It's my impression, although I don't have actual statistics, that in the past thirty years as many as a couple of hundred second-generation employees have been with Holiday Inns at one time or another. I know that it proved personally significant to me when my two sons joined the company. William worked in franchise sales and then overseas for awhile in the Bahamas and Europe. Rusty worked his way up through jobs at inns, and in various departments in the company, to eventually becoming a franchisee himself.

Whatever may be done about second-generation prospects for the work force, it should practically be a rule for executives to put high on their agenda a search for their own successors by deliberately stimulating initiative throughout the company. That's inseparable from managerial excellence. A discerning manager knows that genuine initiative is what separates the champs from the wimps.

That's an incredibly vital distinction to be able to make by those who hold executive responsibilities. Except for a few who see themselves as mere caretakers of assets (what a demeaning vocation!), top managers usually are the kind who want to help their business surge and spread. They remember what initiatives they themselves have had to create or capitalize on in order to advance their own careers, so they know what a powerful motivation it can be to generate peak performance in the next rank of leaders.

How can managers communicate to employees at every level an executive attitude of tolerance for initiative and of support for innovation?

Take for starters the extremely lowly but time-honored device of a suggestion box. Who ever really takes it seriously? What might happen, though, if instead of just setting it in a remote corner of the company cafeteria, you give it a place of spotlighted prominence in a major traffic area in the headquarters building? That would signal to every worker: "The boss wants you to notice this opportunity for you to have your say."

Then, instead of sending a secretary or file clerk to surreptitiously smuggle the box's contents into some executive isolation booth for screening and sorting, try having an officer of the company preside over occasional ceremonial openings of the box, with plenty of attention-getting fanfare and flourish. Whenever an employee suggestion happens to click with management thinking and gets implemented, let the bugles blow while the chief executive bestows badge and bonus with appropriate comments.

The picture may seem exaggerated, but the principle is fundamental. To encourage initiative, you have to provide conspicuous opportunity and conspicuous recognition. It has to be made to *matter* in the company culture. When that gets communicated, employees will go home at night mulling over ways they can improve company operations or products in their own departments, and there actually will be some meritorious suggestions forthcoming.

That simple illustration symbolizes how management attitude can promote initiatives toward excellence. Another key incentive is concern for quality—of workmanship, of product, of service, of representation, of reputation. You communicate that by doing everything in a quality way at the top level and on down. Quality control becomes everybody's business, which means that nobody leaves it to somebody else to maintain.

Each person is responsible to exercise individual initiative—whether by picking up misfired litter around a wastebasket, or by "sharpening the pencil" on a budget proposal, or even by using a competitor's product or service to test its claimed virtues. Managers at all levels who promote high standards of quality control in little matters as well as great ones will breed initiative into the entire work force in their departments.

If handled improperly, all of this can backfire. To load employees with all kinds of nit-picking rules and regulations under the pretense of maintaining standards will suppress initiative faster than anything else. Legalism always fosters hairsplitting over division of responsibilities. Tacking up admonitory slogans all over the walls can rapidly become counterproductive as resentments build.

That's why training has to cover more than mere performance of duties. Initiative thrives best in an atmosphere of voluntarism. Excellent training nurtures a worker's imagination to think up and try out new things.

Initiative also is stifled significantly by breakdown of upward, lateral, and downward communication at any level. I'll have a lot to say about that larger subject later. But it has to be underscored here that company managers and junior executives who feel left out of things are not going to show much spontaneity or creativity.

That surfaced in the 1974 management crisis at Holiday City. It was pointed out to us that communication gaps were causing seriously detrimental consequences for managerial morale and efficiency. There was lack of coordination among departments and divisions, the impact of decisions was not being measured, and informal grapevines were flourishing to make up for lack of official channels of communication.

Confusion flourishes where communication lags. And confused employees are uncertain whether their initiatives will be welcomed or will be held against them.

Whatever is blocking the flow of information needs to be cleared up as quickly as possible, whether that is an executive's mindset or a subordinate's abuse of privilege or a system flaw. The people must know what management is thinking, and management must know what people are thinking.

Another sure killer of initiative is ridicule. Maybe some lowly worker's suggestion in the box or via a memo really is cockeyed. It has got to be gratefully received nevertheless, or other people will feel intimidated and will withhold their perfectly good ideas.

And good ideas are not a dime a dozen. A company that doesn't generate fresh thinking at all levels, that doesn't welcome innovative contributions from employees, will stagnate.

Some will protest that consistency is the virtue to be preferred above creativity. After all, don't people keep buying the brand names they have learned to rely on for consistency? Didn't we in Holiday Inns, Inc., pride ourselves on the fact that our guests anywhere in the world would be in for no surprises when they checked in to one of our rooms? That was the point Peters and Waterman made when they mentioned Holiday Inns in their best-seller, *In Search of Excellence*.

There was a sense in which I really wanted to make this claim: When you've seen one Holiday Inn, you've seen them all. I did not mean by that to force every inn into exactly the same mold. We had two-story inns and thirty-two story inns. Some had revolving rooftop restaurants, and some had palm tree-shaded patios. Some had lobbies or lounges that were straight out of the roaring twenties, while others were a throwback to the Victorian nineties. There was plenty of room for individualizing an inn's appearance and amenities.

But there was no room, I felt, for violating the system personality. Holiday Inns were basic buildings, with basic features, and most of all with a basic Attitude toward the public: Hospitality. Respect for the dignity of the individual. Love for your neighbor.

A guest leaving one of our inns after a stay of a night or longer might not be able to identify a lot of differences between us and our competitors when it came to beds or TV sets or menus or swimming pools. But we always did everything in our power to guarantee that she or he drove away from a Holiday Inn feeling good about our Attitude!

Training, for us, meant getting every one of our 150,000 or more employees throughout the system onto the same wavelength. Our inns might be undistinguished in certain respects, but our people would be like no others in the food and lodging industry. Our family, our company, was our success secret. Through training we tried to help all of them make the most of their God-given talents, to realize their personal potential, while at the same time we faithfully adhered to the corporate image that travelers depended on.

When some old favorite lets the public down, it's almost like a bereavement. They feel they've lost a friend. And in a sense they're right. Besides, there's nothing to be gained by tampering with something that is working fine. We Americans found that out in the break-up of AT&T and in the ill-fated experiment with new-formula Coke!

At the same time, though, even the most satisfied customers are constantly bombarded with appeals and pressures to try a competing product. In market surveys they are subjected to taste tests and touch tests and even smell tests to convince them to switch brands.

To keep consistency without lapsing into complacency, someone in the business organization has to be thinking up and trying out new ways of doing the old thing, or new things to go along with the old that will give it a competitive edge. This is what we call innovation.

Initiative. Innovation. They're like Siamese twins.

Holiday Inns was an innovation in the lodging industry. In fact, when I was going through the throes of organizing the system, I found out in Washington that my task with the government was to patent the features of Holiday Inns *service*, not simply to copyright its name. We were issued certificates of registration for our service mark—the name and the Great Sign—because officials were satisfied what we were offering was different from prevailing industry practice.

Many of our innovations, of course, taken separately, were copied by others almost immediately. When we put in a swimming pool, for instance, there was nothing to prevent the motel across the street from putting in a bigger one with a fancy shape. Even at that, there's a limit to how much you can do with a swimming pool.

Or is there? Not in a company where initiative is encouraged, where the people who work for you are challenged to innovate.

Innkeeper Jack Lawson in Johnson City, Tennessee, got tired of seeing no profitable activity around his motel pool during the winter season. He devised an off-season alternative to swimming: he stocked the pool with trout and then charged his guests for each fish they caught and for the full meal trimmings after he cooked it for them!

Jack's project cleared $745 in five weeks, and as an entertainment feature it attracted and held a number of additional inn guests. One man spent $80 on fish one weekend and gladly paid to have his catch iced down to take home with him.

For awhile we had an affiliation with the Trav-L-Park organization. One of the more imaginative operators was Jule Eldridge in Santee, South Carolina. He devised special events to draw families to his place: in September, a back-to-school weekend; in October, a Halloween observance; at Thanksgiving, an old-fashioned dinner with 100 families, each bringing a covered dish while the park provided the turkey; and at Christmas, nearly 125 families enjoyed an outing there.

Kemmons commented that Jule "created business and didn't wait for times to get better to do it."

As I often said to our people at Holiday Inns, if room renting is our business, we have little to offer travelers that is distinctive. But if we recognize that our business is hospitality, helping travelers to enjoy their stay with us, we'll constantly try to come up with new and fresh ideas to make things interesting and pleasant.

The excellent manager will not be resistant to change. I heard of an old man who once said to a younger, "My friend, there have been a lot of changes in this world in my lifetime—and I was against every last one of them!"

The hardening of the mental arteries at the management level, which is an occupational hazard to be reckoned with, can produce a type of rigor mortis that is the cause of death rather than its effect.

Change merely for change's sake, though, is seldom useful. It's got to be a change for the better. A new concept that raises your sights and makes you stretch to improve what you already do well.

With all of our insistence on maintaining the integrity of the system, we found individual franchise holders and innkeepers resisting proposed changes from time to time that we at headquarters were convinced would improve operations. They refused to vote for them even though, after they were adopted, they were required to go along with the rest of the association's decision.

You can never be sure that every change will hit the mark. If there has been adequate research and testing, however, and if unforeseen problems get worked out in early operations, the overall good of the company is likely to be served.

In management, stimulating innovation among workers

is a never-ending challenge. If executives want their people, on the one hand, to perpetuate the company's already good standing with the public, they must also create an atmosphere that permits imaginative approaches that might enhance the company's reputation.

The potential for leadership in a manager's willpower never shows up stronger than when challenged with a problem. To motivate others, you can't cower and clutch in the face of difficulties. Rather, you launch aggressive counteroffensives to put the opposition off balance and to occupy new territory.

Excellent leaders summon workers to rally and charge. Of course there will be uncertainty about the outcome. Of course the enterprise may incur some losses. Of course critics will snipe and doubters will drag their heels. But through the whole process everybody is going to learn things they didn't know when starting in—and they'll be better off for it even if they fall short of some objectives.

The benefit of problems is to stretch and strengthen a company's coping capacities. At Holiday Inns, Inc., from day one we made some poor decisions and some costly mistakes. Yet we got to be number one in our industry not because everything worked in our favor but because we had sense and nerve enough to keep stepping out in defiance of difficulties.

What I'm trying to emphasize is that executives play the key role in stimulating initiative by the spirit they manifest toward challenges.

Obviously, you can't have everybody in the organization trying out new things every day. But there are some ways to honor and promote creative instincts while at the same time keeping everyday operations on an even keel.

Projects are one useful means. Assign one or more people to short-term, intensive activity on a specific problem so they will be free of routine responsibilities for the duration. If exploration always has to be conducted on the side, while the burden of regular duties remains full, it will only cause a lot of frustration for both workers and management. Flexible personnel assignments, within prudent guidelines, give inventive spirits the air space they need to float their trial balloons.

It may be sad, but it's true that most executives understand productivity much better than they understand creativity. They are oriented toward results and often very impatient with process. If input and output aren't back-to-back, they figure that something must have fallen in the cracks. They want people to work like copying machines too much of the time!

Innovation needs more than a challenge if it is going to pay off. The challenge is merely a launching pad. Management must make sure there's plenty of fuel and a good crew aboard before the countdown begins. And once the team is in orbit, probing possibilities way out there where nobody's ever been before, the monitors at headquarters have to be able not only to send signals when necessary, but also to be resilient to unexpected developments.

At Holiday Inns, we faced one special challenge that threatened to turn our phenomenal success into a fiasco. Inns had multiplied so rapidly in so short a time, and occupancy rates were running so far ahead of industry averages, that we were bogging down on handling reservations. The existing TWX equipment just couldn't keep up with the traffic. Scores of thousands of people every night were depending on our knowing where they were booked and having a bed for them.

What we needed was a computerized reservations system, something not too easy to come by back in the early sixties. American Airlines had just finished installing theirs at a cost of $30 million. We didn't have that kind of money, so we appointed a committee of franchisees and staff people to tackle the project.

Since we'd previously been working with some off-the-shelf pieces we'd bought from IBM, we approached them about our need. They weren't interested in manufacturing customized equipment until, it's my hunch, word got to Mr. Watson that a $5 million contract was hanging in the balance.

They accepted our proposal and sent one of their fine men, Ray Schultz, to work with our Dick Ashman in creating the equipment specifications to do our job. It had to be simple enough so that the average desk clerk could operate it just by pressing color-coded keys.

Other businesses were following the same pursuit as the computer age was coming into its own. At least five that I knew about, including American Express, tried to do what we were trying but eventually gave up and abandoned the project.

We didn't. Schultz and Ashman, along with franchisees like Earl Jones and the good people they picked to back them up in research and design, devoted themselves 100 percent to meeting the challenge. The result was HOLIDEX— possibly the most revolutionary use of computer technology up to that time in day-to-day operation of a business.

It's impossible to calculate accurately the economic value of this development to the company. As one direct illustration, in its first six months of operation in 1965, HOLIDEX processed 4,590,000 messages. On the old TWX that would have cost us more than $3.9 million, but on the new system it cost $1.24 million. The financial rewards accruing to us from heightened customer satisfaction with our handling of reservations were equally impressive.

That was HOLIDEX in its infancy, of course. Fourteen years later I gave an update on it in my address to the American Automobile Association's World Wide Travel Managers Meeting. At that point in time, a spot check showed that during one twenty-four-hour period, the HOLIDEX network processed 950,000 messages.

Such unprecedented volume required the company in 1980 to inaugurate an updated version, HOLIDEX II, at a cost of $25 million and representing the equivalent of 100 person-years in development! By then, we had linkages not only with company and system inns worldwide, but with more than 100 corporations and travel agencies, and with 17,500 reservation terminals of eight major airlines.

A company can be proud, as we were, of people whose initiative and imagination result in such a monumental innovation. In the midst of this rosy picture of super payoffs, though, a stern reality intrudes. There's an extremely subtle danger on the training/initiative/innovation front that lurks like a minefield. It's known as executive ego. Many a fine subordinate has been blown up by inadvertently detonating a boss's pet prerogative or private prejudice.

People get to the top by believing in themselves and by working hard. But once at the pinnacle, they sometimes forget that they don't have all the answers within themselves, and that it's not a crime or a shame to admit it. They've dusted themselves off pretty well from the pratfalls they took on the way up, and now they seem to want everybody to think they simply ascended on high without ever coming in contact with anything common to the rest of humankind.

Such executives are notoriously petty in the arguments

they pick with others and are overbearing in their contempt for ideas they didn't originate. The result is that even the men and women closest to them keep quiet in their presence or fall into the hypocrisy of saying yes on signal, plotting the day of deliverance with executive suite intrigues a Brutus might envy.

Accomplishments notwithstanding, no manager can lay claim to excellence whose ego rebukes or represses the initiative of colleagues. Such administration is the stuff of tyranny. It insures mediocrity or worse.

I certainly was not invulnerable to this malady as I directed operations from my command post at Holiday City headquarters in Memphis. The chairman and the president (Kemmons and Wallace) gave me amazing leeway to exercise my own initiative the greater part of the time. I came into my association with them directly from a decade of successful and remunerative law practice just to be part of their exciting venture.

But, honestly, I wasn't really experienced in doing half the things Kemmons asked me to do in organizing the company. I knelt on a dirt floor in the back of an old plumbing shop that Wallace owned and prayed sincerely, "God, you and I know that I don't know nearly as much as I need to about organizing corporations, much less a hotel business. Help me!"

Years later, I'd still pray for the Lord's help when I drove my Cadillac in from my suburban home to face a roomful of American business moguls assembled at the Holiday Inns home office to discuss big merger deals.

Kemmons didn't know how scared I was (or never showed that he knew), and I never let on to the corporate leaders that I hardly even understood some of their terminology. I kept up appearances and kept quiet whenever that silence would mask my ignorance and talked with vigor whenever I did have something to say—and I got a reputation for being smart and skillful, maybe just a little beyond what the facts would support!

As a result, I began to believe in my image instead of my reality. People saw me as self-sufficient and self-assured, so I began to think and act that way. Especially when I moved up to president, I savored the prestige and power that were mine—by virtue of my own abilities and determination, I thought. So my ego began to get protective, too, and clashes in the boardroom tended to get longer and louder as I defended my turf and expounded my ideas.

Ego and excellence can't coexist for long. Ego intimidates and inhibits initiative, and without imaginative initiative the corporate ship goes aground on the mud flats. It's an ignominious finale to a flamboyant cruise.

One of the sadder aspects of such developments is that the younger managers who had looked to the senior as a model get disillusioned and discouraged. They begin to keep their thoughts to themselves, and the company is the poorer for it. Gloom spreads throughout the corporate family, and before you know it the public gets uneasy and begins to shop around for alternatives. Business erodes. The directors get nervous to the point of panic. Old standards are then set aside in desperate moves to recover.

And the egocentric executive withdraws to lick wounds and bemoan the decline of empire.

I said at the beginning of this book that I wanted to tell you what I've learned about the importance of a good attitude, partly so you would not have to repeat my mistakes. It is hard for me to reveal these recollections, but you are a fool if you don't think long thoughts about what I have said.

The search for excellence starts and ends in the heart of the person who occupies the inner sanctum of the executive suite or any management position.

Whether you head an institution, a corporation, a movement, or some inconspicuous personal enterprise, excellence *is* attainable. I've yet to discuss the ultimate key element in the attitude that underlies it. But at this point I can't pull any punches. So let me put it to you once more as straight as I can: *The more you believe in the rightful exercise of your own initiative to get ahead in business—and you must—the more humbly you also must admit and accept the valid initiatives of others who can help you to arrive at your goals and to survive when you get there.*

The ubiquitous Gideon Bible found in hotel rooms all around the world points out that one member of the physical body cannot say to another member, "I don't need you." Private initiative must be exercised in concert with others' initiatives, or else the body—whether family, church, business, or the social structure at large—will collapse and disintegrate.

On those too rare occasions when I was willing to admit that I was needy, I immediately found helpers all around me. They were glad to be a part of my support system, and I was able to reciprocate some of the time. We held each other up, and the whole was stronger than the sum of its parts. That's the way it should be in the business world, even among executives.

The professional mortality rate among chief executive officers in recent days has been absolutely appalling. Many factors account for it, because modern business is highly complex. But some of the most widely publicized debacles have involved apparent unwillingness by the executives in question to relinquish their personal grip, to take associates into their confidence for counsel, and to encourage new initiatives. What was once excellent leadership has passed into oblivion.

Depth of the management team was always one of my great satisfactions at Holiday Inns. Take Dick Ashman of HOLIDEX fame, for instance. He started with us as a traveling auditor, came into the home office and was groomed as my right-hand man, successfully engineered the computer project, and went on to become a division president.

Jack Barksdale was another. He probably had one of the most enviable records in the company going back to his days in the personnel department as director of industrial relations. But before that, he was an innkeeper, and eventually he ended up being responsible to direct operation of the 300 company-owned inns.

When Mike Rose appeared on the scene as a young attorney with his degree from Harvard University Law School, he was as tough a contender for what he wanted in his inn development division as he was on the tennis courts. I commented on this in my last speech at an annual conference, in October 1974. Just ten years later, Mike was chairman of the board and chief executive officer of the company under its new name, Holiday Corporation.

There were so many of these initiative-exercising people in our ranks that it's a wonder the company could find room for them all. But what a wealth of energy such people bring to any organization that can tolerate and encourage them!

Whether you're still on the way up, or already standing on top, invite others to get into the act. You might not learn a lot from them that you didn't already know, and the company may not make a million dollars off every idea. But your attitude of acceptance creates a nonthreatening atmosphere in which all feel free to participate. It motivates people to stay on the creative edge and to improve their performance by taking all the training you can give them—for the company's sake.

I pity the know-it-all executives whose pride won't let them listen and learn. Employees under that kind of mismanagement will fast become frustrated, and their humdrum performance will show up on the balance sheet. They won't likely complain, because they want to keep their jobs. But neither will they reach personal satisfaction through their work, nor become enthusiastic boosters of the company.

When I addressed the worldwide congress of the European Hotel School Directors in Oxford, England, in 1974, I spent some time describing our various training programs. The goals, I said, were efficiency, effectiveness, and feeling.

Those first two, efficiency and effectiveness, are almost universally agreed upon: the former deals with job skills, the latter with job results.

But the third, feeling, is a Holiday Inns distinctive, rooted in the company Attitude. I'm not using the word in the sense of "emotion," although there's nothing disgraceful about that.

The feeling employees have about their jobs, the intangible spirit that catches their fellow workers and the public they serve, is most positive when there is full opportunity to exercise personal initiative and creativity within the boundaries of corporate policy.

Initiative is the most productive way to get out of a rut. Use your own. Help others contribute theirs, giving them the freedom to chase rainbows once in a while. Make it part of the foundation in any kind of training program you devise.

If you don't, so-called training may amount to no more than conditioning people to jump through hoops in a corporate amateur show.

# III. THINKING RIGHT ABOUT LEADING PEOPLE

# 7. Maintaining Communication
*Will the People Listen to You?*

It used to be that a person's good name mattered more than almost anything else. One could lose fortune and friends, but one wanted to hang onto a good name at all costs.

I sometimes wonder if that standard gets much credence these days. People in government, in business, in the professions, and even in religion seem to go on their merry ways largely unphased by whatever scandals may have been associated with them.

It's not limited to things like marital unfaithfulness, which has become practically commonplace, and which the public no longer seems shocked to hear about. Incidentally, though, popular curiosity about even such matters hints that domestic debacles are still regarded as an exception rather than the norm.

What troubles me is that deviousness, dishonesty, and downright criminal activity have been exposed with increasing frequency in top echelons of management in blue-chip companies. Defrauding our own government and other nations has become a routine way of doing business. Conniving to get around IRS and SEC regulations challenges some of the best minds in business and law.

What this does to a person's name and reputation is viewed by many as of little consequence. A corporate crook either resigns or retires suddenly, taking a golden parachute of bonuses and benefits along, and then is picked up by some other company almost immediately as a consultant at an enormous fee. No one seems to care what has cast a shadow over his name; he's actually admired for what he's been able to get away with and for coming out on top.

When I needed a considerable sum of money a few years ago, I phoned Bob Brock, a business associate of mine in another city, who is also a friend of more than thirty years, to let him know about it.

"I have just one question, Bill," he said.

I thought maybe he was going to ask me what I'd put up for collateral, or what interest rate I'd agree to. I waited a bit nervously for him to go on.

His question was, "Where do you want me to send the money?"

A little later, I was personally pursuing a multimillion-dollar venture and needed an immediate loan of several hundred thousand dollars. One of the leading banks on the West Coast advanced it to me on my signature.

It matters a lot to me to be regarded as trustworthy by my associates in business. I have gone to considerable lengths over the years to protect the value of my name.

During my years with Holiday Inns, I borrowed money from the bank so that I could pick up some stock options that I had coming from the company, only to have the market value of that stock plummet just after the Arab oil embargo in 1974.

I was stuck with a bank debt of well over one million dollars, plus the interest that came due regularly on short-term notes. I waited as long as I could, and then when the stock had inched up a little from its bottom price, I had to sell practically all of it to pay off the bank.

The huge financial loss I took was worth it to me to keep my name clear of any bad marks.

The value of a person's name really was brought home to me with force when I first became associated with Kemmons Wilson and Wallace Johnson. They had good reputations in our community of Memphis and throughout the mid-South, though both of them had the kind of entrepreneurial spirit that prompted them to pursue a high-risk business venture now and then.

But when it came to developing the Holiday Inns dream, they were determined to see it through even if it cost them their shirts. When they proposed that I join them as executive vice-president to put the franchise system together and run daily operations, they were $37,500 in debt on the project and had to combine their resources to scrape together the $500 a month for my salary. Nevertheless, I accepted their offer on a handshake, without there ever being a written contract between us. They had good names.

Early on, we were building an inn in Portsmouth, Virginia, and were desperate for funding to satisfy some creditors there. Wallace Johnson told me one day that he wanted me to go along with him to talk to a bank there about the money.

I was an eager young lawyer, flattered at the opportunity this esteemed businessman was giving me in the fledgling company, so I got busy and dug out all the necessary documents, certificates, records of corporate operations, and resolutions and stuffed them into my briefcase.

After some harrowing experiences while flying to Portsmouth in a little plane, we walked into the bank at last. We sat down in front of the desk of the president, a fine old gentleman with snow white hair. He opened the conversation with some comments about local baseball in his city, and what a crime it was that it seemed to be on its way out.

I don't think Wallace had ever been in a baseball park in his life, but he sat there agreeing with everything the bank president said! They lamented together about the adverse influence of television on local baseball.

All the while, I was sitting on the edge of my chair, clutching my impressive briefcase that bulged with all the necessary documents, the material that the bank would require as security or collateral. I knew that our eggshell corporation wasn't really worth much and hoped the banker wouldn't inspect the papers too closely.

Finally, the old man leaned back and said, "By the way, Mr. Johnson, you wanted what?"

Wallace replied, as cool as you please, "I came in here to get $50,000."

"Oh," said the banker. He called to a man at a nearby desk. "John, make out a note over there and let Mr. Johnson sign it. Put the money in his account here."

Then he turned back to Wallace. "You know, Mr. Johnson, we've got to do something about this baseball situation."

That venerable financier wasn't lending money to a bunch of paper documents, or even to a shaky young corporation. He was putting his dollars into an individual, Wallace Johnson, whom he had sized up by his own standards and rated OK.

Honest lawyers will tell you that you can't draw a single legal document that will serve all purposes to the full satisfaction of all parties. It is ultimately the intent of the parties that will count. Some things you just can't put into writing—and one of them is the reliability of your name.

In a slightly different way, perhaps, the same is true of

a company name. There it's not so much the names of individual management members that the public puts stock in as it is the tested and proven dependability of the company's goods and services. How many times have you heard someone say of a company, with a tone of regret, "They aren't what they used to be; they're just trading on their name."

What does your company name mean to people? Do they swear by it, or swear at it?

Top management is responsible for the company image or reputation, because quality control doesn't begin on the assembly line but in the board room. If the men and women who sit around that polished mahogany table under the scrutinizing eye of founders' portraits on the paneled walls care at all about what a name means—their own and the company's—they will make their decisions accordingly.

I have sat in boardrooms where the meaning of the name didn't matter to everybody. Where "what's good for the business" had to do only with augmenting the bottom-line dollar sign. Where tradition and principle took a back seat to expediency and profit. Where people with good names, personally, compromised themselves professionally by voting against their conscience or by hiding behind a favorite camouflage—abstention.

If American business is to recover its credibility with the American people, who are always disposed to think the best of someone but who are thoroughly disillusioned with impersonal conglomerates that victimize them, those men and women in the boardroom and the executive suite have got to start caring again, really caring about their names.

After all, a name is the metaphor of a person, the symbolic representation of an individual's character. When a name falls into disgrace, it's because the person who wears it has become disreputable.

Managers who strive for excellence by maintaining the right Attitude in their conduct of business affairs recognize that their names are also symbolic of leadership. It is popularly assumed that all top executives got into the driver's seat by more than sheer luck. They had to have something else going for them, some qualities and abilities that earned for them the right to be boss. At least that's the myth.

The reality of leadership quality is subtle but not nebulous. Executive excellence always exhibits certain very tangible and concrete components. At the very top of the list, as far as I'm concerned, is *communication*.

Nowhere is an Attitude of right thinking about people more baldly exposed than in the ways and means managers use to communicate. Too many of them seem to think that they have communicated when they have dashed off their memos. Nothing could be more fallacious.

I heard about an actual situation in Washington, D.C., that involved a writing consultant advising the head of a government agency about a reply to his superior's memo. The consultant suggested that the answer could be much simpler than the original draft.

"Just say," he suggested, " 'Your directive received. Will proceed to comply.' "

"Oh, no!" protested the bureaucrat. "I could never do that. In the first place, I don't even begin to understand his directive. In the second place, a few weeks or months from now, an inspector may come from his department to check on what I've been up to and may find that nothing has been done about this directive."

He paused to gather strength, and concluded, "Unless I reply to that directive in such a way that I have several verbal bunkers behind which I can hide, I'll be out looking for another job. It has taken me years of effort here in Washington to learn how to reply to ambiguous messages with sufficiently ambiguous language to get me off the hook when I'm called to account."

Is it any wonder that paperwork accounts for a large part of the national debt! It reminds me of another apocryphal but plausible case where a government worker received a circulating document, initialed it routinely, and passed it on. A day or two later, the paper came back to his desk with this instruction:

"This was not intended for your reading. Please erase your initials, and initial the erasure."

Ah yes, communicating is a tricky business!

At Holiday Inns, Inc., in our initial dealings with those all-important franchisees, the potential for a divisive force was enormous. Our business idea was a new one, and their expectations were extremely high. At the same time, their experience in their own businesses was rich and varied, and they were not the kind of people who passively accepted edicts handed down from some higher power.

Since our purpose was to unite and motivate that diverse group to work together as a single entity, I kept in constant touch with them through letters and phone calls. The object was partly, of course, to keep them informed of developments right up to the minute. But, just as strategically, I had to communicate to them the very strong and accurate impression that their thinking was vital to us in shaping the organization. Their vote mattered significantly in any company deliberations that would affect their franchise operations.

Ever after that, the franchisees organization, which eventually became the IAHI, International Association of Holiday Inns, felt that their stake in the parent company's success was as significant as our stake in theirs. When their executive directors came to Memphis for a meeting, we always turned over the boardroom to them and hosted them in every way just as we would our Holiday Inns board members. My highest honor was to speak to them at their annual conferences, not so much to report on company affairs as to communicate all over again the vision and Attitude that distinguished our joint efforts to serve the traveling public. Did it sink in and produce results in the way they conducted business?

Not only did the franchisees operate under their own constitution and by-laws, but they also adopted and adhered to a "Holiday Inn Franchise Owners' Code of Responsibility." There, in addition to pledging to maintain the integrity of the system in professional ways, they committed themselves to personal relationships that eloquently echoed the company Attitude.

For example, they agreed to "recognize and treat every franchise owner as an equal business associate," despite wide disparity in size of inns and volume of business. "When we help each other, we help ourselves," the code said.

There was even a clause to "refrain from criticism of another franchise owner to outside parties." It went on to say, "Constructive criticism within the system is a healthy necessity, but downgrading a comember to parties outside the system degrades the organization. Frequently criticism is unwarranted and not based on fact, but once uttered is irrevocable. Frank discussion among ourselves and mutual defense to outsiders are equally helpful."

Those owners had the Attitude because it had been *communicated* to them—made the common possession of all—through the give and take of dialogue and interaction to hammer out agreements between them and the company, and between themselves.

Communication always must be two-way, which means exhibiting the Attitude of respect by listening as well as talking. Too many managers acknowledge this only as an afterthought. They inform but seldom consult. It's essential to truthfully make the people affiliated with a company feel that their viewpoints matter before not after things have happened. We certainly tried to practice that policy with our franchisees, since their system used the name "Holiday Inn" in almost five times as many locations as company-owned inns.

If your business has a plan, ask the people what they think about it. If your business has a problem, ask the people what they would do about it. I found that there are very few things management cannot be open about with employees, especially in a publicly owned corporation.

I admired the people at Delta Air Lines who, when they learned their company was having some financial trouble, pooled their money and bought the company a new plane. That's the kind of employee response you can motivate when you keep the lines of communication open at all times.

When the Sakowitz store in Houston declared bankruptcy in 1985, employees gathered with balloons and banners that read "Mr. Robert, we are 100% behind you." They paid for a full-page ad in the newspaper and planted a tree in front of a Sakowitz store. Is it any wonder that Chairman and Chief Executive Officer Robert T. Sakowitz, according to newspaper accounts, had to take "a moment to regain his composure" when addressing employees?

Expressions like those are the evidence of actual leadership, not just having one's name painted on the president's door or engraved on the corporate letterhead. Authentic leadership is not so much assigned from the top as ascribed from below, from the people who follow—willingly.

Since all the experts tell us we have moved into the information age with the perfecting of computerized data storage and retrieval systems, communications has become a mammoth industry. Even in the media, regional editions of national newspapers are now printed by electronic impulses relayed from satellites. Television is everywhere, telling us all kinds of things we don't need to know and letting us in on very little of what is essential for making wise judgments about human affairs.

In the midst of all this inundation of information, what an old journalist referred to as the "daily glut of occurrences," how can executives get across to their workers their essential messages? Note this, merely getting the word *out* doesn't guarantee getting it *across*.

Perhaps the most important and useful test of communication is what the new technology calls feedback. In effect, the communicator is asking, "What did you hear me say?" In the business world, where molehill messages readily get inflated into mountains of memorandums, it's often hard to accomplish the basic interchange of statement and response.

At Holiday Inns, I established what I called "Breakfast with the President," to which each week I'd invite staff members of different departments—not just the heads, but the support staff as well, as many as a hundred sometimes. The purpose was to make sure that communication was a two-way dialogue. I used the occasion to announce and explain company policies and executive decisions that affected departmental doings and the workers' lives.

But I also made sure there was time allowed for questions and reactions. If we ran out of time, I'd invite them to send their suggestions along to me in a note—and many of them did that over the years, producing some very useful ideas for management to consider.

I suppose I could have conveyed the information in a mimeographed bulletin of some sort. But if leadership is the issue, and I think it is, you've got to demonstrate to your people how highly *you* rate this two-way process. The employees who came to that 7:30 breakfast with me knew that I had to get stirring by 6:30 A.M. and drive in from the country to meet them. That in itself was a message.

How did they respond?

In my personal files are letters and notes of appreciation that came from all ranks of people in the company. Some were typed by supervisory personnel on department letterheads, others were pencil-scrawled on sheets torn from memo pads, not a few came through the mail, carefully handwritten on quality stationery.

One of our department directors said, in his very courteous thank-you note after one of those breakfasts, that "at the risk of sounding 'corny,'" he thought my remarks were "most moving," and that many men and women in his area had relayed to him their favorable impressions. He was a veteran employee who knew me well, but he valued the chance for broader sharing of the Attitude within the ranks and spoke of "the real blessing we have in being each a *real* part of the 'Family.'"

He expected the impetus of my comments to produce long-term good effects in his staff, he wrote, and then concluded with, "we are proud to follow a leader like you."

I confess it is comforting to get a message like that. But, complimentary as it may be to me, it underscores a far more vital point: People are more disposed to follow someone's leadership if the contact is personalized in some way.

From an employee of Holiday Press came this variation on the theme: "I am very proud to be a part of this family and work in Attitude Country." She listed twelve things she appreciated that the company did to make employees feel the family spirit, ranging from profit sharing to a complimentary subscription to *Guideposts* magazine. Her closing comment was most gratifying: "These past ten years have been interesting, exciting, and challenging, and I can hardly wait to get to work in the morning. I love it here."

A handwritten note from another Holiday Press woman made another point:

> This morning was like living next door to a nice neighbor, for years always speaking and being very cordial, but this morning was like that neighbor I had known and liked took me by the hand and said "I'm glad you are my neighbor."
>
> Holiday Press, it has been said, is the step-child of Holiday Inns, and many times I've felt this is true . . . but what you did this morning and will be doing for many Tuesday mornings is telling us we are no longer a step-child . . . Thank you for keeping the Holiday Inn Family a big happy family.

I tried in vain to get some of the other people in the executive suite to participate or to duplicate the activity in their own area. They thought that this weekly meeting with the *hoi polloi* was a waste of time. Their usual response was, "Now, Bill, that's your job. You go ahead and do that."

I maintained then, and still do, that listening to the people whom you expect to listen to you is the best investment of your time.

Furthermore, you've got to learn their language. Effective communication always has to begin on the receiver's wavelength. If I'm so preoccupied with the supposed importance of what I have to say that I don't bother to translate it into terms my hearers can identify with, I'm wasting my breath. Worse, I'm frustrating their desire to please me by following through on what I ask of them.

There's another angle to this besides listening to feedback. Not everything that goes on in a company requires dialogue. I always welcomed occasions when I could simply get in touch with the people to let them know that management was thinking of them.

At Christmas, for instance, I would send a seasonal greeting to the entire system over their HOLIDEX machines. It would be transmitted over 300,000 miles of voice-grade lines (we were AT&T's largest customer) and be picked up in every one of the nearly 2,000 inns we operated around the world.

This HOLIDEX capability for me to override all other computer messages with the push of a button had to be used sparingly, of course, so as not to disrupt our vital reservations processes. But it represented an executive privilege that symbolized a willingness, at least, to communicate, to touch people with a word of good cheer.

At corporate headquarters in Holiday City, I could do the same thing in a little different way. We had music piped in through all the offices, which I could interrupt with a button push to deliver a special message to the entire work force there. Again, it gave a chance to let them know that we upstairs were on the job, too, and were aware that they were doing their best.

We did the same thing through the printed media. The first issue of *Holiday Inn Times* was dated January 1, 1956, a humble effort indeed, with the mimeo stencil cut by my wife, Geneva. We reported current items on inn construction and franchise expansion, so that everybody working for us could share the excitement of company growth.

And you better believe they took it seriously! I had people writing me letters of protest: "Hey, you left *me* out. I'm doing so and so." They wanted to be recognized as a part of what was going on.

To make sure we didn't skip anyone thereafter, we designated one person in each department, division, and subsidiary, as well as every inn, to be responsible to funnel information to the editor.

What they sent were people stories full of human interest. We reported marriages, new babies, honors, bowling league standings, individual awards, company advancements, features on families, chaplain's reports, and outstanding company programs that everyone could take pride in.

We also boasted of the number of inns and rooms open and operating to date, both company-owned and in the franchise system. There was a running score comparing previous figures. Major stories told of innkeepers and staff people who were recognized for doing the best job.

Always the tone was upbeat and forward looking, and always crediting the people themselves with the company's phenomenal gains. "What YOU are doing is almost unbelievable. A business miracle! Keep up the good work. Your company thanks YOU!"

This periodical generated tremendous esprit de corps and gave people a real sense of belonging to the family, even if they were working for us as far from Memphis as Europe or the Orient. Whether it was a stockhandler or a stockholder, we felt they were fully worthy to be informed about company matters.

That's the togetherness I tried to create in all of our communications efforts. What good did it do for me to talk about family if there was not a real sense of belonging to each other? By communication, our commonality was given

tangible expression, constantly reinforcing the company Attitude. It may have been *the* main driving force that caused
the young corporation to excel. It was like the spirit of the
Three Musketeers: All for one, and one for all.

Again, I am sensitive to the charge that we were a sentimental set down here in Memphis, running a business as
if it were a family. Well, let me give the critics a little more
ammunition! I put communication with employees on a decidedly personal basis—I mean one-on-one—through the
assistance of our chaplain's office, when I sent the president's
best wishes on birthdays, weddings, anniversaries, arrival of
new babies, and children's graduations. We established recognition of "Teenager of the Week," and "Teenager of the
Month," and other kinds of honors.

These certainly weren't chores that I had to do, nor
would they ever have found their way into my job description had such a document existed. I loved every minute of
it.

And people can tell when you do. There's nothing they
can see through faster than insincerity and hypocrisy—a mechanical routine of ThankYouThankYouThankYou. Your
little attentions to them, done out of a genuinely thankful
heart, do more than anything else to lift them out of the
work doldrums of a nine-to-five treadmill.

We believed in communicating to shareholders and the
public, too, of course. As soon as each year's annual report
was printed, the mailing process began—to news media,
financial magazine publishers, banks, colleges and univer-
sities, and even to government officials here and in every
country where we were doing business.

In this publication, too, I exploited the human relations
potential, filling the pages with pictures of individuals and
of groups at work in company operations. I sent a copy to

the wife, husband, or family of company people, as well as to each franchisee. With it went a personal cover letter from me thanking each member of the company, and especially the spouses for sharing their loved one with us.

It's not hard to imagine the sense of worth generated in responsible individuals when their pictures were in the annual report, their accomplishments reviewed, and their commendations publicly recorded. I felt, and still feel, that is one of the finest opportunities a company has to motivate its people to give their best. And when they are doing that, you can be sure both public and shareholders are being well served.

Today, unpleasant as it may be to admit, too many corporations are preoccupied with pandering to the financial institutions and with pacifying stockholders instead of motivating their own people. That's shortsighted, even stupid.

Despite the usual criticism that we were too homespun, and despite eventually turning over that publication job to outside professionals, the Holiday Inns, Inc., annual report for several years won first place in its category of awards given by financial magazines. More recent issues have suggested quite a different image of the company that must correspond accurately to the changes that have occurred there.

Once you have communicated faithfully to your own people inside the company, you must let the general public and the professional world know what the company stands for and what it's accomplishing. It's a part of stewardship responsibility that goes with a free enterprise opportunity.

Communication has to be done in person, too, not just through electronic and print media. I developed a regular speakers' bureau among the executive staff, division and department heads, and subsidiary representatives, who went out and made speeches at colleges, chambers of commerce, service clubs, tourism conventions, and state and federal meetings. It was not enough to keep our story before the public and the special groups. We needed to keep our people before them, too.

A corporation, no matter how personal it tries to be in its messages, remains pretty much a disembodied abstraction until people can identify it with a face and a voice. To tell the Holiday Inns story, which I dearly loved to do myself, I intentionally sent other executives from time to time for a couple of reasons: (1) I wanted to expose the depth of expert management that we had at the company; and (2) I wanted the executives themselves to know that I trusted them to do a good job and to be a credit to their company when they were placed in the spotlight of public attention.

There was another fringe benefit to all of this public communicating. Long before the days when the government had to enact full disclosure regulations to force candor, we were trying to level with people about our situation. That wins a lot of goodwill and confidence. The legal department at headquarters hassled me constantly about this openness, but I think that they overreacted and too strictly interpreted certain SEC restraints. It's old-fashioned to say it, I know, but I do believe honesty is the best policy.

Managers who want to be excellent in their professional performance can never get away from my thesis that Attitude, thinking right about people, is foundational.

For me, there's no profounder justification for this thesis than in those ageless words of good news from the New Testament: "God so loved the world, that he gave his Son . . ." (John 3:16).

Commenting on that verse, a translations expert, Dr. Eugene Nida, has observed: "All divine communication is incarnational." That's a big mouthful of theology for a layman like me to chew, so I'll go with the simpler version: God became human.

And what was that becoming all about?

Communication.

After all the prophets and patriarchs and the priests and poets had told about God's plan for humanity's salvation from self-destruction, God sent Jesus to work it out in the flesh. I view that as the supreme communication event of all time.

I'd like to venture an exercise in adapting the mystery of all that to a practical outline for business.

In Jesus, I see communication exhibited as talk put into action.

1. The message is formulated in terms that the receiver is familiar with, so the receiver can relate it to what she or he already knows.
2. The message is relayed by someone who understands both its content and its intent and also understands the setting in which the receiver lives and works.
3. The message is designed to get the receiver's response—a simple yes or no.
4. The message is intended for the receiver to relay to others.
5. The message is specific in spelling out exactly what effects will follow from putting it into action.
6. The message is backed by the full authority of the sender.
7. The message is guaranteed to improve the existing state of things if applied according to instructions.

You can adapt that outline with a slight revision: just

substitute the words *executive order* for *message*, and you'll have a whole theory of communication for daily business operations. (For me, by putting the name "Jesus Christ" in that spot, I have the basis for my relationship to God, now and forever.)

Executives, like anybody else, can be confident that they have communicated successfully only when their intended result has been produced at the other end. Was the message acted on? Did it make the difference it was supposed to make? If not, was it the fault of the sender or of the receiver?

If it was the fault of the sender, was the order not transmitted clearly? Did the sender order the impossible? Did the sender not know the score in the first place?

An excellent manager will ask questions like these so as not to misjudge the person who received the message but did not comply.

If it was the fault of the receiver, does the sender understand how it impressed the receiver? Does the sender know the circumstances the receiver was in when the message came? Does the sender have the insight and intelligence to reissue the message so that its reception will be improved?

An excellent manager, with the right Attitude about people, will not be quick to blame somebody else for faulty reception of messages but will assume personal responsibility to see that his or her meaning does eventually get across, even if it takes several tries.

Keep in mind that the root meaning of the word *communication* is "common." For a message, or a piece of information, to be held in common, it is necessary that what belonged to only one party at the beginning belongs identically to both parties at the end. A lot of what passes for communication these days misses that objective completely.

One person talks without translating, while the other listens without understanding, and the whole effort is wasted because what was said is not what was heard.

A mediocre executive will say in such a situation, "Well, it's the other person's responsibility to figure out what I'm saying."

An excellent executive with the right Attitude will say, "I've got to find some better way to help the other person understand me, so that we can work together to get our job done."

Respect for one's neighbor. The Attitude. It's the added dimension that makes the difference between motivation and manipulation.

A breakdown in communications is really a breakdown in human relations. No amount of technological tinkering with media will succeed in getting the message across if the people involved lack a common ground.

# 8. Handling Authority
## Will the People Respond to You?

Running a close second to communication in the criteria of leadership is authority. Many people would put that one first, I suppose, because it is so often construed as a synonym for leadership. But if a person can't communicate effectively, no amount of authority or control is going to compensate sufficiently to create a productive enterprise.

You hear a lot of current talk about centralized and decentralized approaches to organization and administration. At Holiday Inns, Inc., we practiced strong centralized policy control and decentralized operational responsibility. Under that arrangement, changes could originate anywhere, but they had to be tested and reviewed via staff to executive committee to board and sometimes to shareholders.

Decentralization meant that we put people in charge who were closest to where the action was and thus were in a better position to manage it. We had utter confidence in our well-qualified management team and felt no hesitancy in delegating responsibility to them.

Since excellent management of a business can spring only out of a motivational attitude toward employees, I need to translate those cumbersome words into people terms. For me, *centralization* and *decentralization* are as dry and unproductive as Death Valley unless they are irrigated from a deep well of humane concern.

To put it into human talk, then: centralization has to do

with authority, and decentralization has to do with autonomy.

From infancy onward, the whole human experience is lived in the tension between those two—authority and autonomy. On the one hand, we need and want points of reference, principles we can depend on, constants in the midst of never-ending change. People value authority.

On the other hand, we must have room to breathe, flexibility to make our own moves, the exhilaration of risking and winning. People demand autonomy.

Put those drives into the context of a modern business and you've got tension for sure! It can tear the company apart with dissension and divisiveness.

I've been a participant in some boardroom brawls that would do credit to a zoo. It doesn't seem as if any of us ever outgrow the "My way vs. your way" controversy. I've seen top corporate executives bare their teeth at each other in confrontation and then go yelping off in different directions afterwards to lick their wounds in private. I've more than seen it. I've done it. It can be viciously painful when authority and autonomy lock horns in a business combat.

Are we doomed to everlasting repetition of this violence? Is this simply the way things are, and nothing can change them?

To some extent, yes. We have to admit that there's something decidedly flawed and unholy in human nature, even though we are made in the image of God. That something is vain ambition, according to the Bible. Not the drive to achieve, which is God-given and good. Rather, it's a distorted drive to achieve supremacy over others, a devilish determination to be the almighty one.

Vanity does not make for constructive reconciliation of differences between people. Yet executives, of all business managers, seem most susceptible to that base instinct. By the very nature of their exalted position, they are bound to relish authority—the power to make people do things, and to make decisions that shape events—even if that's only the course of their own company.

Everyone wants to leave a mark for the future to notice. If nothing else, graffiti in the subway will do.

By the same token, the higher managers rise in the hierarchy of a company, the more they relish autonomy. They've gotten to levels where they don't always have to ask for permission to act. They have executive privilege. They bark, and everybody jumps. For them, at long last, their authority and their autonomy have combined in a heady mixture that readily induces intoxication of the ego. And because they want to hang onto everything they've fought so hard to acquire, they are passionately reluctant to allow much autonomy in the subordinate echelons of management. They give lip service to the principle of initiative, but they bite their fingernails if evidences of it become too conspicuous within the ranks.

Probably the hardest job in the world is to convince top managers to share authority and to promote autonomy. Two truths have to dawn on them.

First, their authority is, at best, both limited and temporary. Their word might be law within the company, but it doesn't reach far beyond that.

Second, their authority gives them a unique vantage point from which they can spot and encourage the brightest and best among younger associates and apprentice them to carry on the things they believe in after the senior steps out of the picture.

Such realism and farsightedness can help to relieve some of the tension an executive feels personally, but how to align the authority and autonomy poles in business so that their magnetic field is productively charged is another challenge.

At the risk of being simplistic, I'd like to suggest that the single most important factor in resolving the authority/autonomy problem is accountability.

People in business understand very clearly the implications of that word in the financial arena. They staff whole departments with accountants and auditors to make sure they have every dollar they think they have, and that they actually are spending those dollars where they think they are being spent, and that they actually are solvent and not bankrupt!

When I was deputy chairman of the board of directors of the Federal Reserve Bank in St. Louis, I served as chairman of the personnel committee and as a member of the audit committee for six years. I was on the advisory committee to the Board of Governors of the Federal Reserve in Washington. I know how stringent the regulations are, and I know how scrupulous the monitoring must be.

Front-page headlines in recent years have told one horror story after another about big business, including big banks, that have floundered or foundered because some people in the organization weren't as accountable as they should have been. More often than not, that lack of accountability has been in the executive suite and has included even the board of directors.

Where a whole lot of executives go wrong, I think, is in failing to see that in business the accountability of authority is first downward. They are constantly peering upward at the directors or outward at the shareholders with a neurotic obsession to satisfy expectations in those directions.

In reality, though, their prime responsibility is to instill *within* their own company ranks an unmistakable awareness of its purposes and objectives. What is its reason for being, its justification for existence in a crowded and competitive marketplace?

Ernest Breech, who had a fantastic record of rebuilding corporations, emphasized the need to communicate to all levels of management in order to minimize criticism stemming from people's ignorance of reasons behind policies.

Unless employees perceive the essential worth of what their business is all about, how are they ever going to give it their last full measure of devotion? A person in authority who wants loyalty from people can't get it by commanding it to be given. It's got to be generated within them out of conviction that loyalty matters.

A corresponding responsibility is to make clear to employees what top management expects them to do individually and collectively in order to fulfill company purposes and goals. "What in the world does the boss want?" is not an uncommon question in the ranks of a business.

Executives sometimes let themselves get so remote from the realities of daily operations that they mandate what's both impossible and impractical. They seem to forget that they are required to keep on top of the company situation in more than title only. Otherwise, they'll never be able to convey the challenges facing that business in terms the workers can relate to and do something about.

Don't think I'm underestimating the degree of accountability executives have to their shareholders. It's enormous. It is the investment of those people that gives a company significant working capital. Executives must answer to them, as stewards of their funds responsible for the highest possible return through the wisest possible use.

As one of our top officers put it one tense day, eloquently if not elegantly: "Who do you think I answer to—

40,000 mad stockholders, that's who, and I don't intend to make any more damned excuses to them."

Nevertheless, a company makes a tactical mistake when it puts shareholder accountability as top priority. That leads to an untold volume of trouble internally and harms public relations.

The reason is simple enough to analyze: if dividend per share is what matters most to management, it will be tempted to do almost anything (in fact, you can strike out the *almost*) to satisfy that goal. The "anything" can range from compromising product quality to exploiting employees to falsifying the books.

The departure from founding principles at Holiday Inns was, in my opinion, attributable more to pressure from major shareholders to increase company earnings and their personal dividends, than it was to internal or market factors.

And the "anything" that a company will do under such circumstances may undermine its accountability to its public as well, the consumers of its product, the users of its services. What's good for business isn't always good for the people whom that business is supposed to be serving. Holiday Inns and I came to a parting of the ways over that very issue—but more about that later.

For the present, though, to summarize: executive accountability is wide ranging in its expression and effect. It touches workers, investors, consumers. Accountable managers know that their vested authority—whether over a whole corporation, a division, a department, or just a committee—does not give them almighty autonomy in wielding power irresponsibly. The satisfying of others' interests is a major part of the harness they wear in pulling the load entrusted to them.

But most of all, accountability touches the executive individual personally. In the inmost sphere, it goes deeper than one's reputation as a moral person or an efficient manager. It gets to the heart of the matter: feeling good about oneself. I'm talking about self-respect, not self-adulation.

Everyone who has a bad self-image is destined, sooner or later, to mess up in relationships with others. That leads to broken communications, thwarted goals, depressed morale, and some form or other of self-destruction. In that order. Ironically, the whole inner mess is too frequently masked by a bravado that is mistaken for self-assurance.

One sure symptom that something is wrong is an executive's unwillingness to ask or accept help. Being the authority figure in any operation prevents admission of need, some seem to think.

Would an innkeeper facing a personal crisis, for example, ever seek counsel from a maid? From the franchise owner, maybe, or someone at headquarters—but surely not from the person who strips dirty linens from the beds and scours toilets!

Would an executive in a plush penthouse office ever admit desperation or despair to the messenger who carries the executive's communiques throughout the corridors of empire? Who wants to hear "the lonely whine of the top dog," as one observant pastor describes it?

Being at the peak of the pyramid does not allow much room for anyone to stand beside you. But does such isolation really go with the territory of authority, or is it induced by something else?

By pride, maybe? Must one at the top never admit to any uncertainty or vulnerability? That's ridiculous, and everyone knows it.

By fear, then? Can someone at the top be readily displaced by an ambitious young understudy who actually does know the right answer to some nagging professional dilemma? That fresh insight should be welcomed as rewarding proof of the executive's good character judgment.

The higher some executives climb up the corporate Everest, the more they tend to want to go it alone. What are they trying to prove? That they can live without the oxygen of human fellowship? That they can survive without the supply line of timely advice from below?

A wise sage has said, "If you want a man to be your friend, let him do something for you."

Management excellence perceives the company as filled with gifted individuals who are not threats to authority but are companions in the crusade, and whose gifts can be drawn on humbly and fearlessly. Executives who do this will more likely endear themselves to their peers than earn scorn.

Administrators who admit to themselves and others both the limitations of their power and the scope of their accountability will not trip over those delusions of grandeur that are the best-concealed booby trap in the executive suite. Remember, I'm saying all this with the wisdom of hindsight. I'm not claiming that while I was in top management I was always sensitively alert to these dangers myself. I'm not just pointing fingers at other people with whom I had disagreements and battles. I'm sharing what I learned— some of it from disillusioning observation, and some of it from painful self-discovery.

Only when an executive man or woman successfully strikes the balance between their authority and their autonomy by a sensitively calibrated personal accountability are they ready to administer a business properly.

Accountability, though, like communication, is definitely a two-way street. Those in top authority are obligated to enforce accountability in the ranks below them. The welfare of the company, its general health, is in their hands. If they do not require upward accountability from subordinates who have been allowed certain latitude for exercising their own autonomy, everybody will be in trouble.

Autonomy is liberty to act within limits. It is not absolute. It is not license to do anything and everything.

One of our officers said, "We've had to hold back competent people, some with really superior abilities, because they simply couldn't get along with their coworkers. . . . We know that a man or woman who works extra well with others at their level will probably be able to get those people to work well *for* them as well as *with* them. This is how we pick our executives."

Wise top executives may allow others a long leash and hold it lightly, but they invite disaster if they let go altogether. There is indispensable need to require upward accountability.

This might not always be as definitive or measurable as the downward kind, because the dynamics at work are sometimes less observable. But there are certain safeguards against autonomous extremism.

Setting goals is one. The free-spirited experimenter should be responsible to somebody to outline what she or he hopes or expects to discover or develop. There must be a business-related validity, a sensible purpose in every project. Executives must evaluate how it fits into overall corporate strategy.

Another safeguard is a timetable. While voyages of discovery cannot always be strictly calendered, provisions are made to last for a specific length of time. And while estimated time of arrival at the destination cannot be pinpointed exactly, there must be interim progress reports. Managers must follow closely what is going on in an area where many unknown factors can surface or a situation may become unmanageable.

Those required reports, whether in writing or in conference, are extremely important when it comes to the Attitude of respect for people that constitutes managerial excellence. If they are properly requisitioned, they will convey to the project director this message from the supervisor: "I'm eager to learn from what you are discovering. Do you have any news?" This tone eliminates the "I'm keeping an eye on you" impression and boosts the integrity of the experimenter.

It doesn't, however, eliminate the agreed-upon proviso that further authorizations down the line will be contingent on satisfactory reports, adequately documented. A blank check too often leads to extravagance. Autonomy without accountability breeds waste and wingdings!

We had a special situation with regard to autonomy in our vast network of franchise owners. Maybe a good term in this connection would be *participatory autonomy.* I think this statement by one of our officers summed it up well:

"They have to live up to a set of standards, which assures a good operation, but they help set the standards. We all put a part of our revenues into a pool for national advertising, but we all help determine the amount that goes into the pool . . . The company gets a royalty from the franchise, and in return the company makes sure that everyone maintains the standards . . . But—and this is really important—as long as the franchise owner adheres to the system's standards and policies you have a high degree of autonomy, but you also have many of the advantages which are usually confined to large corporations."

If a solid sense of accountability, downward from and

upward to the executive office, is part of the company Attitude as it should be, the inevitable tension between authority and autonomy will have a much better chance of
being constructive and productive. The tension is unavoidable, but Attitude makes a difference in the outcome.

When a company talks about "centralized this" and "decentralized that," therefore, it must be in those human terms
of who is responsible to whom for what and why. Just to
contrive an organizational chart that divides up duties is too
mechanical. It does not reckon with the drives at work in
people or with the business pressures under which they exercise those drives.

Excellent executives enjoy the exercise of authority and
encourage the exercise of autonomy with equal good humor, since they know that their respect for the dignity of
persons will help to motivate sincere accountability from
others. It will generate not only harmony in the ranks but
also appreciated value to the shareholders and satisfaction to
the public.

Do I have to admit at last, though, that all of this is so
much starry-eyed idealism? How can we strike that delicate
balance between authority and autonomy when the prevailing system of cutthroat commercial competition challenges the highest historic principles of ethics and morality?

That's an extremely hard question. The answer is not
simple. But the answer is clear.

Take authority first. You begin to understand it correctly
when you are under it, long before you are given much of
it. In the home, traditionally at least, the authority of parents
has given children a good object lesson that the other side
of the authority coin is submission. Anarchy knows no authority. To put it another way: authority is meaningless if
no one obeys it.

The issue is not essentially managerial, but spiritual. Supreme authority belongs only to God, who made us in his image, and who governs our lives from our first to our final breath. Someone has to be in charge of earthly affairs, of course, and God has ordained that to be our human stewardship ever since his creating of the race.

Secularists deny any authority higher than human, of course, declaring that ethics are situational and morals are relative: everyone has license to do whatever seems right. This is the antithesis of order and management.

Ironically, even a democracy carries a hint of that tone in its ideal of *vox populi, vox dei*—that the voice of the people is the voice of God. As interpreted and applied in American tradition, however, that is not an anarchical thought. Rather, it emphasizes that the united voice of the people exercises checks and balances on the voice of just one person. The consent of the governed is a precious heritage to us, and we must do everything necessary to preserve it as our legacy to coming generations.

There's an even greater safeguard, though, to our liberty. In this populist democracy of ours, we do officially recognize a higher authority in many statements. "Under God," we say in the Pledge of Allegiance to the flag. "In God We Trust," we say on our money. All of the arguments about separation of church and state cannot gainsay the well-documented historical fact that our founding fathers were God-fearing men.

What does all this have to do with business management in a modern setting? Just what it has to do with leadership in any other realm: no man or woman will entertain illusions of personal divinity when they acknowledge one who is higher than they. Business executives today, as in every generation, will comprehend the authority that is theirs only to the degree of their own experience of submission to authority—both human and divine. In the mystery of paradox, the truth is that authority flows from submission.

Consider a railroad locomotive, for example. It is designed and fueled to transport heavy trains over long distances. Whether that train ever gets anywhere is up to the engine that is powered to pull it.

But whether the engine itself gets anywhere is dependent on the tracks. An off-the-track engine is free, no longer restricted to those two narrowly confining rails. But it can't go anywhere while it's off the track, and can't fulfill its destiny of pulling the train.

The tracks that limit a locomotive are the tracks that liberate it!

Quite contrary to indicating weakness, then, submission to rightful authority is strength. It's smart, too. That's well known to anyone who ever said "Show me how" to someone who knew how.

Believe me, I found that out a hundred times over in my business career, as well as before and since. Ever since my boyhood, when my grandmother impressed on me indelibly that God would help me when I needed it, if I would just ask him, I've been a firm believer in taking him up on that!

Here's the way I found it to work for me. In those early years at Holiday Inns when we were developing so rapidly and entering into multimillion dollar agreements with leading American corporations like Gulf Oil, American Express, IBM, and others, I found myself plunged into negotiations that were way over my head.

I was only a night school lawyer with a fairly unimposing ten-year practice behind me. As I would drive into the city from my home on days when we had important

sessions scheduled with chief exective officers of big businesses, along with all their sharp financial and legal advisors,
I was scared.

So I prayed.

"Lord," I'd say, "you know and I know that I don't
fathom everything about these deals I'm getting into today.
I'm up against some wily pros, and I've got to see that the
best interests of Holiday Inns are taken care of. Please help
me! Give me the wisdom to make the right decisions and
the courage to carry them out. And remember, Lord," I'd
add (not really knowing him well enough at the time to
realize that he didn't need to be reminded about anything!),
"all that I do in that meeting today I want to do for the
glorification of your kingdom. Amen."

That was submission to authority. Not because I was a
particularly pious or humble person, but because I was desperate. It taught me that God isn't all that fussy about our
using fancy words and phrases, or even about our making
requests with totally pure motives. What he wants is our
trust, so that he can show us what he can do.

Well, he showed me. Time after time, I found, the ner-
vousness and panic I felt in anticipation and the actual ignorance I had about what to do were replaced in the meeting
room with an unusual calm and self-control and with a sur-
prising capacity to cope in the give and take of technical talk
around the conference table.

If belief in God isn't just lip service, a kind of Ameri-
canized civil religion that one wears like a class ring, then
I can tell you from my own limited experience that God
does hear and answer prayers. Not because we are good and
deserving—which we're not—but because it's his nature to
be forgiving and kind.

I've had my share of personal struggles with ego and

power, but I can honestly say that I've never truly believed that I was self-sufficient for all things. It doesn't hurt my feelings to admit to a higher authority than myself, even though I aspired for years to cap my career by wearing the title of chairman of the board at Holiday Inns.

A lot of the things I did in my executive capacity that were seen as religious by my colleagues and the public were merely reflections of my conviction that we are all under authority, the rule of God, and that as the Bible says, we are to walk humbly before him.

Rebellion against divine authority was original sin. We are living with the resultant chaos of that disobedience, both in the natural realm and in the human spirit. That's why the authority issue is so problematic. Conscience still tells us to rebel against injustice and indecency, while our instinct for self-justification finds us putting up with unjust and indecent elements in flawed earthly systems without protest. The tension between acquiescence and resistance is a daily business crisis.

My point is this: executives, who hold so much authority and autonomy in their office, can compensate for their mortal vulnerability to abuse of power by a daily reaffirmation of faith in the one who is higher, by a "declaration of dependence" on a source of strength and wisdom above and beyond their own. That will help to keep them in their place, under authority, at the same time that they responsibly wield authority in their business.

If you refuse to be under, you can never successfully be over. In fact, it's my conviction that if you do not have a submissive attitude before God, he will take away your authority. Ancient King Saul is a tragic case of that, while his successor David, by no means a perfect man, nevertheless pleased the Lord through his humility and obedience.

The Bible constantly amazes me with its pertinent commentary on such matters. In a column he prepared for the *Holiday Times,* Chaplain Nance quoted these words from the Apostle Paul in Ephesians 6: "And, as for you employers, be as conscientious and responsible toward those who serve you as you expect them to be toward you, neither misusing the power over others that has been put in your hands, nor forgetting that you are responsible yourselves to a heavenly employer who makes no distinction between master and man."

I have never felt that submission to God was embarrassing. I do not believe that it demeans, but that it exalts. If you lean your weight on a fragile stick and it snaps, your tumble is humiliating. But if you lean your weight on someone's strong arm and are upheld, your standing is glorious. The difference is not in you, but in your support system, and the outcome of your dependency is what matters.

Any leader who refuses to submit to authority is never going to be able to convince others what is meant by submission to authority. That's why managers in particular need to acknowledge some authority over themselves. It's the only way they will understand the psychology of submission, which they try to instill in workers for the good of all.

You can only teach what you have learned. You can only model what you know how to do. To defy this principle is like driving north in the southbound lane of the expressway. Your freedom to do your own thing in your own way will come to a smashing conclusion!

If you obey the laws, though—the authority of the highway engineers and the traffic patrols—you will get where you're going in one piece without having destroyed anyone else enroute.

The executive attitude toward managerial power that wins worker loyalty esteems authority as a privilege, not as a right. Responsible executives see themselves as trustees, not as tyrants. While they do possess awesome leverage in their final yes or no, they don't exert it simply to bolster their own ego or to line their own pocket.

Sometimes I think the energy potential that gets wasted at the executive level in business and industry is more than our natural and nuclear fuel resources combined. It appalls me to observe the losses we have suffered in leadership capacity for our society, not through inept management—of which there is too much—but through self-serving practices by those who should be secure enough to get over that.

It might not be so tragic if there weren't so much at stake. But what goes on in many executive suites and corporate boardrooms across the land today reminds me of infamous Nero, strumming his lyre and making up intolerably egocentric ballads for the applause of his fawning courtiers, while on its seven hills along the Tiber his imperial Rome burned to ashes.

You can find that sort of narcissistic nonsense among many people at the top, and not just in the business realm. I've seen it in the United States Senate hearing rooms, and at Federal Reserve Board committee meetings. I've sat through the same routine even in churches and religious organizations, where the last thing you might expect would be self-centered calculations governing policy and program.

I'm not proud to admit that I've been a party to this at times. As I look back on my business career from the vantage point of retirement, I can detect a scar or wart here and there on my nice-guy image. In fact, perspective shows me now that I may have been more of a scrapper than I thought. Every once in a while, for instance, I had showdowns with the chairman of the board that were real donnybrooks. It would be face-saving if I could claim that every battle was over some righteous principle, but it wouldn't be true.

Like every executive, I suppose, I was jealous of the prerogatives of my authority and touchy whenever my motives or methods were called into question. That's only human, we say defensively; we might be high and mighty on the social scale, but we all have feet of clay.

My point is this: executives, vulnerable though they may be to universal human foibles, have a professional mandate to subordinate self-interest for the general good. They are to use their authority to benefit the maximum number in maximum ways.

One reason why working people—both blue collar and white collar—resent management people the way they do is that they see right through executive hypocrisy. Whenever they find those rare administrators who demonstrate that their walk matches up to their talk, they will do their best to be cooperative and constructive.

If your employees know that you have a reputation for issuing beneficial orders, for biting the bullet on hard decisions in favor of honesty and fair play, for contributing at some cost to worthy needs where there's little or no likelihood of repayment, and for exercising your power to advance what's right over what's convenient, then they are going to be motivated to support your leadership.

Then they will point with pride whenever your name gets into the newspapers for some professional accomplishment or some community service. Then they will become the best public relations people you can find to promote the products or services of your business.

Unenlightened managers, who constantly make power

plays just for the thrill of flexing their administrative muscle, are wasting an incredible reserve of leadership power.

Excellent executives, on the other hand, who wield their considerable influence to make things happen that will create a better life for a lot of people, are channeling a force into society that will help to shape history. The executive echelon will never lack for committed support from below as long as it treats its authority as a sacred stewardship.

True leaders are not simply the ones in front. They are the ones who show the way.

# 9. Modeling Love
## *Will the People Commit to You?*

The way.

Top management people in business, industry, and the professions often feel like blind leaders of the blind. If there's one thing they are *not* as sure of as they want and need to be, it's the way.

Impenetrable jungle or trackless desert loom ahead, the sky is dark with no stars to guide them, and every customary compass they've relied on in past situations seems to have gone berserk.

What can they do? Play their hunches, maybe? Use a trial-and-error approach? Or settle for waiting it out until some kind of dawn breaks?

Those options don't sit well with real leaders. They're the kind of people who like to keep moving toward clearly marked objectives, inspiring the workers to follow them in faith. It frustrates them to be stymied.

I'm going to propose something now that such people have got to take seriously or forfeit their leadership claim. It's such a simple thing that you have to have to be childlike in your trust of it. I've been talking about it for all these pages, now, in one way and another, but here's where it all comes together.

The way *is* the Attitude.

And the Attitude, to put it plainly, is love.

That's not a word in vogue in graduate schools of business administration. It's not a marketplace cliché, by any means. It probably disgusts, or even scares, a lot of narrow-minded executives who can only conceive it to mean soupy or saccharine sentimentality.

The love I'm talking about, though, is a tough commodity—dynamic and demanding. It's not moonlight-and-roses romancing that courts employee response. Rather, it's the most comprehensive discipline any human being can submit to, and executives who can muster the grit to accept it are going to find out, to their likely amazement, that it's also the most pragmatic policy for business efficiency.

This kind of love has a lot less to do with the emotions than with the will. It's not instinctive or impulsive. It's deliberate and determined.

As I understand it, there are four great loves available for all of us to enjoy: love of work, love of country, love of family, and love of God. They are not a smorgasbord from which we pick the one we prefer. They are better pictured as four interlocking gears that make human relationships run smoothly. Dislocate or strip any one of them, and the social machine breaks down.

It's logical to begin with love of work, since that's practically the underlying assumption in executive thinking. A passion for working in general, and a special devotion to the kind of enterprise you're responsible to lead, are indispensable to success and satisfaction.

Kemmons Wilson was a hard worker and proud of it. "I enjoy work," he said on one occasion. "I had rather work than almost anything I know of. I start early and stay at it late, six days a week. I still can cram an awful lot of activity in a working day."

If you love your work, it's a sure thing that you cannot

be a clock watcher. The job you have to do fascinates you any hour of the day or night, and the passing of time goes unnoticed when you're in the thick of things.

I loved working at Holiday Inns, Inc. It never deteriorated into drudgery. Quite the contrary. The heavier the challenges at the office, the higher my zest rose. With all my heart, I believed we were at the very center of a modern business miracle, and I didn't want to miss a single beat.

Executives who feel that way about their business are going to find the challenge to motivate employees is more than half met. Enthusiasm is contagious. It spreads like an epidemic as long as top management lets it be seen and felt throughout the ranks.

When that happens, going to work each morning, leaving home behind, doesn't hang over your people like some inescapable blight on their lives, but rather draws them like a magnet—pulling at some inner urge within themselves that craves to contribute to the excitement of what's happening in the company.

That assumes, of course, that job placement is correct for the individual in the first place. Naturally, someone is not going to be motivated to excel when shoved into a slot where potential is blocked. Even at the managerial level, where giving orders seems to be the basic job description, people sometimes are saddled with line-of-duty obligations that chafe and frustrate.

Being associated with Kemmons for twenty-five years at Holiday Inns as his chief operating officer, I may have had more chance than most people to observe him closely. He had the absolute spirit of entrepreneurship if anyone ever did. Administration was no fun for him, even though he obviously took delight in wearing the title chairman of the board and chief executive officer. That was one of the rewards for his vision in starting a business that became so historically successful.

Even after more than twenty years at the helm, Kemmons still could say, as quoted in *Business Week:* "I have never claimed to be any kind of administrative man at all. It kills me. I hate detail work."

At meetings of the executive committee, of the board, and even of the shareholders, he almost always would merely call the session to order and then turn the gavel over to me to run the meeting. He didn't have much patience with protocol. He much preferred flying off to some remote wide place in the road, or even to an exotic foreign destination, to scout possible sites for the locating of yet another Holiday Inn. Quoting the *Business Week* writer: "Last week Wilson took off for a swing through the Mideast doing what he likes best—making deals."

It was just in his nature to explore and discover and develop, letting others follow his trail with tidying up the legal technicalities and the organizational details. (A person who gets so much fun out of business responsibilities maybe isn't really working in the sense that most of us think of the word!)

On the other hand, I probably was lucky that Kemmons kept on the go so much, whether in behalf of Holiday Inns or one of his many other business ventures. It left me free to do the very thing that I enjoyed to the hilt: to administer day-to-day operations of the corporation with a fairly free hand. A chief operating officer shouldn't complain about that!

If you try to come up with a list of the most incongruous associations of terms you can think of, this might well be one: employment and ecstasy. Who in their right mind would ever put such concepts together? Yet it was my own experience, and I judge it to be the experience of many others, that job satisfaction can be one of the most delightful engagements known to the human species.

Someone has even dared to suggest that it is when we are working that we mortals are most godlike, because we are causing something to come to be that never before existed in quite that fashion. If there's any truth to that, then a very powerful word comes into play regarding work: *vocation*.

When we come across that term in a religious context, we know it means "calling." The implication is that someone in a religious vocation has a divine summons to obey. I like to think it is just as valid to use it to describe daily work in any honorable profession. If God takes an interest in the activities of his creatures, as I believe the Bible teaches he does, then why can't we assume that he directs us into that employment through which we earn a livelihood?

The Quaker philosopher Elton Trueblood expressed this truth most eloquently in a book he wrote decades ago titled *Your Other Vocation*. We are called to our daily work, and it is ennobling to our own spirits as well as to others to go about our business with a sense of divine appointment. Love of work, then, becomes one kind of legitimate responsiveness to God, just so long as we understand clearly that dedication to a job isn't the same thing as religious devotion, nor does it earn merits with the Almighty that will atone for our sins.

While I really do love work with every fiber of my being, it bothers me no end to see so many executives in business who are virtual slaves to their job. They are first at the office in the morning and the last to leave at night.

Some of them even sleep in the office on nights when they've been chained to the desk until very late.

Such people get a lot of credit for being devoted. In my opinion, they are more likely to be distorted. Anybody who eats and sleeps the job is hardly a balanced or healthy person. Something will have to give, sooner or later. Somebody besides the person involved usually has to suffer for it. I know.

In those halcyon years when Holiday Inns skyrocketed to the top of the industry, I usually left home at six in the morning and got back home at ten at night or later. My wife and four children had to shift for themselves. I hardly ever saw them, much less had time to sit down and talk with them or do things together with them. My job was my joy, and whenever there was a family crisis, I sort of resented it as an intrusion into what my life was really all about, as I saw it.

Ironically, of course, I was all that time promoting the idea at Holiday Inns that we were one big happy family. As I think about it ruefully now, I guess I was one of those men who epitomized the expression "married to his work." I walked all over our headquarters complex at Holiday City and flew all over the country to visit our inns just so that I could pat people on the back and smile and tell them what a great job they were doing to make "your company" prosper. But my own boys and girls at home didn't get a hug or listening ear or a helpful word from me every time they needed it.

For that matter, neither did anyone else outside of Holiday Inns. The job consumed so much of my time and energy that I discontinued practically all social contacts with old and intimate friends I'd known since boyhood and school days. Parties at my house or elsewhere, trips, even so-called "vacations," were work-related at least ninety-five percent of the time, as I entertained business associates and visited business locations.

This obsession with work, particularly with one's job, has several drawbacks as I see it now.

First of all, it leads to what I'll call proprietorship toward the business. I didn't own Holiday Inns, Inc., but I ran it with such unceasing oversight and involvement that it felt as if it belonged to me in unique ways. It was "my" company, the employees were "my" people, the goals were "my" goals, even though I tactfully chose to use the second person—"you" and "your"—in all my statements.

An attitude like that can produce side effects that you never intended and that you don't recognize until it is too late. For instance, if anybody ever picked an argument with the way Holiday Inns did something, I took it personally. This sensitivity and protectiveness often deprives you of benefiting from perfectly just and useful criticisms.

Another side effect, obviously, was that I took it personally whenever anyone objected to my proposals or resisted my efforts. Resentment and anger are the stuff of demoralization for those who harbor them and for the people around them. While I kept issuing official pronouncements about Attitude, our company philosophy of respect for the dignity of all people and the Christian guiding principle of love for neighbor, I couldn't help but identify my opponents as enemies and develop an unconscious demeanor of belligerence.

Another drawback to work obsession, besides this possessive proprietorship, is the dislocation of other values. I do believe work is very important not only because it supplies our livelihood, but also because it offers opportunity for self-fulfillment in the exercise of certain gifts we've been given. It's one way of meeting our fair share of responsibility to enhance the well-being of the human race. At that level, work is noble.

But work is not *all*-important. It has its place in life, but it must be kept in its place. That's where executives are particularly vulnerable to disorienting their priorities. Their role is so elevated and their performance has such far-reaching consequences that they begin to get an illusion that the destiny of the human race depends solely on them. While acknowledging theoretically that other aspects of life are important, too, in practice they deny the fact by sacrificing those things to the job.

Upside-down priorities are hazardous to health. With all the things we have to do, we'll tear ourselves apart if we don't get them in the right order. The problem is that there are some things we like to do better than others, regardless of their relative importance. Those favorites tend to sneak toward the top of our priority list. Then, in occasional bursts of conscience, we try to compensate by a rationalistic rearrangement.

That may be the explanation of why some executives mistakenly end up with their work as their top priority. They've almost conned themselves into thinking that the job has to be the first love. They go at it early and late, until every other legitimate claim on their time, energy, and affection ends up in a tangled heap at the bottom.

I've heard them argue that this devotion to duty is unavoidable—at least temporarily—so they can stabilize the business or underwrite the family's security. They say it's a necessary means to better ends.

What happens in many cases is that forces beyond their control unsettle even a well-established business; a spouse pampered with things but deprived of caring attention walks out; children seek their guiding light in a cult or a commune. Executives who are lionized by their peers and the public for their success face themselves in the mirror each morning and ask, "Where did I fail?"

The answer to that lies with priorities. Not with responsibilities. Not even with opportunities. But with values. One reason it is so urgent for executives to get straightened out on this issue is that they cannot motivate the people who work for them primarily by leaning on them with managerial efficiency.

Motivation spreads by the infectious Attitude they have toward the components of personal wholeness: values system, family relationships, role in society, and contribution to human betterment.

The people at work want to know a manager as a person. I didn't say as a "personality," which is simply the way someone comes across to people. I didn't say "personally," because that's usually impossible on a one-to-one basis in any sizable business operation.

The *person* comes through in the Attitude, which is an expression of priorities. It's fairly easy for people to tell by surface signs whether you are healthy, wealthy, and wise—but that's not enough to motivate them. In fact, that may be an intimidation.

What really gets to them, though, and stirs them to strive for excellence within their own maximum capabilities, is evidence that you are devout, loyal, caring, and helpful. People are always looking for heroes. Whether we want to admit it or not, executives by their very prominence are candidates for that role. They may pass inspection on the professional level without any debate; but it's on the personal level, in the conveying of their Attitude, that their motivational influence is most forceful.

Finally, the most subtle pitfall of all can snare many executives who have an obsession with work. They get to thinking that they and the job are one entity, that what they *do* is what they *mean* as a person. Already suffering from a considerable loss of objectivity through possessiveness and misplaced priorities, they cannot think of their own being apart from the job.

Why do so many men, especially, die in the very first months of their retirement when all physical indications are that they are still in their prime and could enjoy a good many useful years ahead? I'm neither a psychologist nor a physician, but I would wager that with their career behind them, as they see it, the meaning for their existence vanishes. Life has lost its purpose simply because they no longer are doing what they did best and enjoyed doing for the previous forty years.

When people can recognize themselves as individual souls only by the external trappings of their temporal activities and pursuits, they already have died, even though the heartbeat and brain waves go on. They have mistaken form for substance. When the familiar form disappears, they think nothing is left.

"My job has been my life" may sound like a triumph, but it carries the sting of tragedy. The workaholic executive is, as the old ballad phrased it, "more to be pitied than censured," because he or she has been taken in by delusions and left empty.

Work will never be the first priority for an excellent executive. I felt that my wholeness as a person was fractured when the time came that I was no longer influential in controlling the affairs of Holiday Inns, Inc., and that it was nearly destroyed when I was out of the picture with no involvement in operations whatsoever. Everything in me lashed out against that reality, and I struggled to regain my lost life in some substitute way. I always had believed myself to be a man of the utmost integrity, but my addiction to my job had upset my balance and left me broken.

In my scale of values now, I would place the love of one's work at the bottom of the list. That's not to diminish its urgent importance; it surely remains one of life's priorities—but a subordinate one. There are higher considerations than the job.

Love of country, for instance.

I'm not suggesting that if you had to choose between labor and patriotism, you should unthinkingly choose the latter. I'm just trying to give a reasonable basis for ordering priorities in terms of their relative value.

Think of it this way: in a totalitarian dictatorship, love of country is really a moot point. So is a choice of job and of the workplace. Under such a system, citizens exist solely for the service of the state as things to be manipulated and exploited for whatever they're worth, and when they're no longer worth anything in the state's estimation, they're dumped.

In a free society, such as we enjoy in America, there is both the atmosphere and the opportunity for me to find a job. To be sure, we have the chronic problem of unemployment, though the recent percentage has been gratifyingly small compared to many other nations. Ideally, we'd like to see full employment all the time, if that meant that every able-bodied person of working age were self-supporting and satisfactorily providing for dependents. But we all know that unemployment statistics, like other figures, usually are whatever each interpreter makes of them, and they will never go away despite political campaign promises.

The point is that I need to give high priority to supporting and defending the kind of governmental system that allows for free work choices, for a chance to advance, and for the liberty to enjoy the results of my labor. If it weren't for those marvelous guarantees of our democratic Constitution and the Bill of Rights, what kind of meaningful employment could I hope for?

The phrase *free enterprise* is almost a redundancy. You can't have the one without the other. As a system, it must be understood as opportunity, not opportunism. In the first, many benefit; in the second, only one or a few. The system as we know it in this country shows the incentive power of being a team player rather than a mere cog. United effort draws on individual knowledge and ability combining with the whole to make something work. The individual who contributes to also shares in the group achievement.

In a free society, where human enterprise is largely unregulated by external authorities beyond minimum social necessity, personal dreams can be pursued. A "patriotic" executive, therefore, communicates to employees the importance of cherishing and protecting liberty as the working environment that promotes self-realization. It is surely in the enlightened self-interest of business to instill workers with a spirit of ambition to prove what they can do, what they can gain, and what they can become, as well as the altruistic spirit of what they can give to insure such liberty to their children.

That was why, in my report to the company president on January 24, 1979, reviewing our position on public and governmental affairs, I urged encouragement of employee political activity and nonpartisan company efforts to motivate employees to a fuller participation in the governmental process as voters and as supporters of a political party and of candidates for office. I also felt we should develop programs in political and economic education to improve employee understanding of our American system.

I am well aware, painfully so, that in recent years the incredibly vast bureaucracy that we call Washington, D.C., has invaded our privacy more and more and increasingly threatened our personal privileges. The American people have understandably protested and have urgently insisted on some dismantlement of it all. Regulatory agencies, both federal and state, have done an astonishing lot to cripple free enterprise. Tax structures in many states have driven businesses out of business. The people's reaction against all of this has registered in elections, because we still believe in government by the consent of the governed.

I think business is obligated to pressure for bureaucratic reforms based on sound operational theory. Beyond such commendable critiques as the Grace report, advocating realistic economies in federal expenditures, we need to volunteer constructive and creative counsel to agencies to help reduce the degree of scandalous mismanagement.

At the same time, however, I also stated in my 1979 report: "The company believes that it is wrong for business to complain that it is misunderstood by government when in fact business has made no real effort to communicate with government its views, thoughts, and recommendations concerning matters affecting its interests and the interests of the people. It is difficult to fault the official if business has not kept him supplied with all of the necessary information which is pertinent to his reaching a favorable conclusion."

But what eternal vigilance it still takes to preserve freedom. Men and women have died to keep us free in the wars of this century, and patriotism has run high at such times. In between, though, recession and inflation and recovery and deflation, in all of their cycles, have wrung us out and tempted us to turn over some of our prerogatives of citizenship to any strong authority that offers a promise of straightening things out.

There are ways in which the business community has been guilty of setting us up for authoritarian takeover. Whenever business creates or significantly contributes to shifting the burden to federal or state governments, it is ultimately the taxpayer who is victimized. And when taxpayers are hurting, they look for saviors.

Consider the crucial issue of wasteful spending. All of us who earn wages and pay bills try to keep a careful eye on what we purchase. A dollar's value for a dollar spent is our perfectly reasonable expectation.

Yet the government, as a purchaser, is bilked out of billions of dollars every day. By whom? By American businesses with whom it has contracts. The scandal of overcharging the government is not just some nasty mess way off in Washington, centered in that favorite Congressional scapegoat, the Pentagon. Its effect comes down to less soup in the pot on every kitchen table in America.

One of the cardinal sins that we continually denounced and fought against at Holiday Inns, Inc., was price gouging by isolated local management. We were a "nice" company, run by "decent" people, with a good image in the public eye. But our inspectors constantly brought back reports to the home office of instances where the public had been taken advantage of by some innkeeper or franchisee because of local circumstances or seasonal fluctuations.

Fair pricing was not only a company policy, going back to Kemmons's original concept. It was an essential part of the Attitude: respect for your neighbor. Whenever you are guided by the principle of charging whatever the market will bear, you are not thinking right about people.

An innkeeper or owner could rationalize that his or her pricing was in line with rates elsewhere or the inflationary impact—what convenient smoke screens those are! But if the price wasn't fair to the traveling public, including business people and families, we were stern enough about it to warn such an inn that we'd remove it from the system and take away our name and sign from the premises.

We did that in some cases. You see, when business compromises the principle of fairness with its customers and they begin to catch on to the distasteful fact that they are being mistreated, right away the natural impulse is for them to turn to the government to police the situation and reinstate justice. "Redress of grievances" it used to be called back in the Revolutionary War era. If a business does not discipline pricing practices on its own initiative, the people can be expected to seek help elsewhere.

But when the customer is the government and business is disposed to take all it can get, the taxpayer is virtually helpless. Let's face it: how can the national debt ever be reduced or the national budget ever be balanced as long as those same businesses that average citizens buy products and services from every day on Main Street are scandalously gouging their biggest customer on the banks of the Potomac?

But candor requires a tougher question even than that. If businesses are prospering through government contracts at ridiculously inflated prices, what workers in business are going to want to see their paychecks reduced because their company is cutting its prices to the government?

Love of country is a whole lot more than flag-waving

and fireworks. It's fair dealing in the marketplace, both by business suppliers and by worker-taxpayers. High taxes taken out of my paycheck by a government that is charged high prices by the business that pays me high wages so that I have to pay high taxes—who can possibly be winning in this vicious game?

Let's translate love of country into some sound and ethical business practices that will get government off the fiscal torture rack so that, in turn, average citizens will have more resources to purchase the goods and services of those businesses. Attitude will make all the difference.

I place a very high priority on love of country, of this free country in particular, because it gives me a chance to survive and to succeed through the unregimented exercise of my own gifts and determination. But my love must extend beyond oratory to action.

When I first went to Washington to represent Holiday Inns and later the travel and tourism industry more broadly because of the Arab oil embargo and the resulting energy crunch, the Secretary of Commerce talked to me sternly. I was trying to convey to him that the government was badly misguided in classifying tourism as a nonessential industry during the crisis. That ruling threatened to put us all out of business—and our business, as I saw it, was to serve the public good.

His retort to me, in effect, was, Where have you been all these years?

I respectfully answered that we were in the hospitality business and didn't think that Washington political actions were really any of our affair back in Memphis.

Secretary Dent got up out of his chair, pointed a bony finger at me, and let loose!

"Mr. Walton, let me tell you something. You'd *better*

get involved in politics, and you'd *better* participate in the governmental affairs of your country, or one of these days your country might not be here!"

I listened. Sooner than I expected, the chance came to get involved far more directly than I'd ever imagined possible—and with a vital service to the government that directly benefited the people of the United States.

After attending an energy meeting in Williamsburg, Virginia, I was disgusted with all of the buck passing between federal agencies and the oil companies, complicated by the intractability of shortsighted environmentalists. So I went back to Washington with a boiler full of righteous indignation.

I made the rounds of several key senatorial offices and other spots on Capitol Hill, finding a sympathetic ear from Dan Inouye of Hawaii and Mark Hatfield of Oregon, among others. At last I wound up face-to-face with the energy czar, William Simon.

In our conversation he emphasized how much gasoline could be saved if motorists would observe the new 55-mile-per-hour speed limit. I promised him on the spot that we would enlist all our innkeepers nationwide to encourage that compliance by putting up slogans on the marquees of their Great Sign outside each inn.

I had another proposition to make to Bill Simon. Our sophisticated HOLIDEX computerized reservation equipment kept us in instantaneous contact with every inn in the system. I suggested that we use it to monitor the entire United States to spot-check the available gasoline situation in each local area and to relay that information to the government. The idea elated him.

Literally overnight we had supplied the Federal Energy Administration with a HOLIDEX machine, and the whole monitoring process became a workable reality—simply because one particular business found a way to serve the government that gave it the freedom to operate at a fair profit.

I would plead with corporate executives throughout the nation to recapture their service motivation and give the government a break. That would lower the deficit and demonstrate that democracy is both workable and desirable.

I can illustrate that very specifically out of my own business context. One thing we must do is to keep the people in Washington better informed. What we had not communicated effectively to our legislators was that tourism in the United States is the second largest industry in our national economy. I tried to correct that information gap through frequent testimony before Senate committees.

At last, a travel and tourism industry advisory committee to the Senate was established, and Senator Inouye appointed me its first chairman. One of our long-term goals was to see a Secretary of Tourism added to the President's Cabinet. We worked with the legislators for several years on this effort, making three tries to get the presidential signature. A major breakthrough came in 1984 when the U.S. Travel and Tourism Administration was authorized at the undersecretary level in the Commerce Department.

Was all this activity prompted by unabashed self-interest on the part of us tourism officials, or was it genuine regard for the national welfare? Let this fact lend its due weight: American travelers had been spending $12 billion a year overseas, while foreign travelers to the United States were spending $4 billion here. That figures out to an $8 billion annual trade deficit in that sector alone.

By contrast, we in the Advisory Council have been exploring ways to turn that around by a promotional program that might bring as much as $18 billion a year into America through foreign visitors. They will get their money's worth not only when they tour this magnificent land of ours, but especially when they encounter the free spirit of our people, which could well be the envy of the rest of the world.

Incidentally, my experience in Washington prompts another idea. Holiday Inns, Inc., had released me from daily company responsibilities and had sent me to the capital so that our case could be made with the government. In the process, however, I and my industry colleagues were able to put at the government's disposal a wealth of professional expertise at no cost to the taxpayers.

Executives who are facing or entering retirement should give serious thought to volunteering a year or two of service to the government, contributing their wisdom and managerial know-how. Instead of fossilizing on some subtropical beach, where all they do is play golf in the morning and party at night, with gin rummy and cocktails in between, let them set up shop in Washington for a short term or on frequent visits—not as those expensive consultants who are known around the capital as the "Beltway Bandits," but as patriotic citizens returning to the country the benefit of business experience that the country gave them the chance to enjoy for so many years.

Even as the Peace Corps took hundreds of American volunteers overseas to lend a helping hand in developing countries, why not recruit an Executive Corps to help bail out the bureaucracy? Excellence should never be retired!

Love of country can find expression right on the doorstep of a business, too, of course. When I referred earlier to my impatience with the environmentalists, I called them "shortsighted." I did not mean to make a generalization condemning all who are concerned about the quality of our life settings. There is very legitimate cause for alarm among all of us when we see the rape of nature that has gone on largely unchecked for so many years in this land where God has given us such an abundance of beauty and resources. We're paying an awesome price for our bad stewardship of such a trust.

At Holiday Inns, committed as we were to providing the traveling public with congenial surroundings for their overnight stops along the highway, we developed a sensitive corporate conscience about the environmental problems. Although we didn't use the word *ecology*, we cared about clean air and related concerns.

Our inspection department included regular examination of inn grounds in each location to see that the outside appearance was attractive, with suitable landscaping. This was not only for eye appeal, but for the general physical and mental health of employees and guests.

Our company's safety engineers worked with innkeepers and their maintenance staffs at various inns to install better equipment that would meet standards of state and city antipollution committees and control boards. In the high-rise Holiday Inn/Rivermont in Memphis, for example, we developed an afterburner for its incinerator that would reduce the fly ash and burn up dirty leftover materials that might pollute the atmosphere. We did constant research on programs to reduce the grease buildup in our kitchens.

At Innkeepers Supply Company, we sold not only garbage disposers and trash compactors and glass crushers to our own system and the industry in general, but also conducted research to examine incineration products that could be installed in other buildings besides motels.

An important Holiday Inns subsidiary, the Johnson Furniture Company in Grand Rapids, Michigan, was notorious at one point for having one of the worst smoke problems in the city. Kemmons later reported:

"The firm converted its boilers—which burned coal, scrapwood, and sawdust—to a forced-air system that keeps sawdust in suspension above a fire fueled by natural gas. Effectiveness of this pollution control measure was dramatically illustrated recently when one of the neighbors asked if the company's boilers had been shut down!"

Another benefit he identified was that "firemen who used to man the boilers around the clock now act as plant guards and help in manufacturing in addition to their regular duties."

Obviously, a concern for the environment, which is one application of the love of country priority, can easily be in a company's own best interest. That's why as another project Holiday Inns, Inc., commissioned an hour-long television documentary on ecology produced by Show Biz, Inc., in Nashville, with Paul Ott singing the title song, "A Message to Mankind."

Love of country, then, can find expression in decent behavior in the local community where a business is located and can extend all the way to state and federal legislative halls. But there's an even greater extension of the principle: the international scene.

Executives committed to love of country as one major priority will do whatever they can to see that the way they conduct their overseas operations reflects the very best in American values and traditions. Unfortunately, however, the newspapers carry almost daily disclosures of American business transgressions in other countries. It's really a sordid picture that should shame us all.

What was it that best-selling book of several years back

called us? The "ugly American." Is any business enterprise doing honor to this "land of the free, and home of the brave" by earning such a designation? Why can't top management realize they do a disservice to both themselves and this nation through practices that are at best often clumsy or stupid, and at worst are criminal?

Holiday Inns branched into international operations very early in its history, eventually spreading to more than fifty countries. I can't compute how many thousands of miles I've flown all over this globe to visit our installations. We officers had opportunities to fraternize with foreign business and governmental executives. We even occasionally entertained heads of state or official delegations at Holiday City headquarters.

I saw all of this travel and contact as fantastically good for business, of course. But there was another dimension to it. The people Attitude is right at the heart of international relations. President Eisenhower launched what was called the People-to-People program. We called our effort "World Understanding Through Tourism: One Road to Peace."

Ambitious? You bet. More than that. Impossible! What's the fun of trying less?

Since what we were all about was hospitality, whether in the United States or on foreign soil, all of our basic corporate principles were equally valid everywhere. We had to say it in different languages and serve it through different menus and style it for different cultural preferences—but the message was always the same: People matter most.

You can't tell me that doesn't pay, if we must resort to commercial terminology. When the diplomats gather around treaty tables in the conference rooms of world capitals, they don't have anything going for them unless they respect each other. International agreements are not worked out successfully by enemies. I sometimes dared to think that we could have resolved some of our world tensions among nations faster if the ambassadors had convened their meetings in deck chairs around a Holiday Inn swimming pool!

The point is that ultimately it's people who have to learn to live at peace with each other, not governments. And in our business we had an almost ideal opportunity to help people get together in a relaxed, nonthreatening atmosphere where they could at least begin to lay the groundwork of better mutual understanding and cooperation.

Our peace program respected the national distinctives that make each people special. We weren't trying to promote some kind of homogeneous human race where everyone was stamped out from a common pattern. The diversities among peoples are exciting and enriching. They must be preserved and appreciated. Even within our own continental boundaries, we are increasingly impressed with the benefits as well as the tensions of a multicultural society.

The American business community urgently needs to rethink its overseas posture and performance. "Yankee go home!" is a terrible rebuke to representatives of a land that in so many ways is the envy of the rest of the world. We don't have territorial ambitions to plant the Stars and Stripes on the soil of other nations, whatever some of our adversaries charge. But we should be aggressively creative about ways to plant the dream of self-help to self-fulfillment in the hearts of the world's peoples—if we believe in it as much as we say we do on the Fourth of July.

The way is the Attitude. The Attitude is love—for work, for country.

And love for one's country means simply to enhance its reputation in every way possible from local community to distant lands. An excellent manager is one who is enlightened about this and who activates it through every channel the business can make available.

Devoted as we should be to our country's good, there is a yet higher priority in the striving for excellence. This gets into a touchy area that many executives resist facing squarely.

This priority is love for family.

What I have to say about family has a whole added dimension to it today that didn't take up as much of our thinking in the executive suite some thirty years ago as it probably should have. Tens of thousands of women worked in Holiday Inns, both at corporate headquarters and throughout the system, and we sincerely tried to take into account some of their special needs. Whenever awards time came around, they were right up there with the men receiving recognition and honor for jobs well done, many of them occupying supervisory positions in a variety of departments. In the franchise system, several women were among our earliest owners of inns, running them as independent businesses with great success.

The place of women in the workplace has changed radically in these decades, though. Positions have opened to them in business and the professions that were once the exclusive domain of men, especially at top and middle management levels, and their leadership capacities are not debatable.

I don't have to look outside my own home for first-rate examples, as I have depended through the years on the business skills of my dear wife, Geneva, to handle the complicated accounts of our household and several auxiliary Walton enterprises. Now both of my daughters are beginning their careers in business. I have to admit, though, that for an old school Southerner like me, the situation has forced me to rearrange some long-held and hard-set patterns of thought.

The fact that there are so many households today in which both parents are wage-earners outside the home confronts modern corporations with a challenge to initiate policy changes that for many of them might be little short of revolutionary. Frankly, I don't know what the best solutions are going to be in the long run, but one concern remains uppermost in my mind amid all the necessary changes: home life must not be allowed to suffer further strains than it has already been subjected to, and *business management must share in the urgent responsibility to help workers build solid and happy families.*

All kinds of suggestions are advanced on this subject, and it's encouraging to see that experiments are going on all over to address the serious problem of America's mushrooming population of "latchkey kids" who have to come home from school every day to parentless houses.

Among ideas that I've heard about are these: letting a husband and wife team split one full-time job wherever that might be possible; allowing paternity as well as maternity leaves; rearranging working hours so that parents can be at home at crucial times of the day to do more parenting in those hours the children need them; or increasing wages and benefits for part-time work, maybe by shortening the work week or lengthening vacation allowances.

Just that brief list of possibilities should be enough to galvanize some entrepreneurial soul in executive management today to engineer exciting modeling of ways that a corporation can help its workers keep priorities straight by putting family nurture higher on the value scale.

When I think of all the things Kemmons introduced into the Holiday Inns concept that were prompted by his personal family concerns, and that did as much as anything else to justify our plea to the government for a "service mark" that distinguished us from the others in the hotel industry, I don't doubt for a minute that the same thing could be done again by other visionaries in other fields under today's fast-changing circumstances.

At least they could if they had sense enough to draw upon the stiff gumption of a business partner like Wallace Johnson had in his gifted wife, Alma, who in the formative days of Holiday Inns was responsible at one point for keeping the whole precarious venture afloat by an investment from her own funds! Alma, and Kemmons's mother, Doll Wilson, probably have never gotten the credit they deserve for making the two partners stick with their dream until it materialized.

But radical rethinking about family priority and rightful business reorientation to the indispensably shared family roles of men and women are going to require the kind of executive strategizing and bold-stroke board pacesetting on some corporation's part that will make today's American business community sit up and take notice just the way we did in 1955. This doesn't mean that the company itself will become either patriarchal or matriarchal in its relation to employees and their families, but that it will do all it can to be a partner with parents who work for it.

Who, I wonder, will be the first company president, or chairperson of a board, who is going to have the courage to say: We believe in the home as a national bulwark, and we're going to see to it that our personnel office gives our employees full cooperation in assuring their children the kind of guidance and sense of security in the home that will grow them up to be proud and purposeful citizens?

The prospect of what that could mean to our national

future is enough to make me wish I could start all over again!

But as the old man said when the minister started talking about chicken stealing: "Now he's stopped preachin' and gone to meddlin'!" For some reason, people in top management develop a dichotomy in their self-perception that separates the personal from the professional. They object that even their own family is a personal matter that has nothing to do with business.

Oh no?

It's my belief that the most devastating problem facing our country, and possibly the world, is the breakdown of the stability of the home and family. And it is of more than passing significance that the Patty Hearsts and Richard Hinkleys of recent memory have come from highly affluent executive homes. The prominent leaders in business or in any other field are bound to be under public scrutiny in every aspect of their lives by reason of their sheer visibility. If they are a success in the marketplace and a failure at home, it raises questions. Executive families as well as employee families are crying for attention.

In the days of my legal practice, whenever it was my task to qualify jurors for a trial, I'd always ask the prospective jurors some questions about their attitudes toward marriage and their relationships to spouse and family. I was not trying to pry into private affairs. Rather, it was one way of determining how serious people were about the solemn vows they take. If they regarded the marriage pledge lightly, there might be some basis for doubting the sincerity of their oath-taking in court.

Like anyone else who is an enthusiast for his ideals, I got to be known around the circuit for certain speeches that were often repeated through the years. Probably people got

tired of hearing them, but I never got tired of making them!
And whenever I might have considered dropping one of
them from my repertoire, some unsuspecting soul would
come along and tell me how the things I had said meant so
much to him or her just at that point in life, and I'd be
reassured that the message could still bear repeating.

One of the devices I used that became famous in its own
way was the marriage vow. I went to Jeb Russell, my minister at Second Presbyterian Church, and asked him for a
copy of the little white booklet that he always read from in
wedding ceremonies and then presented as a souvenir to the
happy couple afterwards. To this very day, I will pull that
out on certain platform occasions and read directly from it:

"I, John, take thee, Mary, to be my wedded wife . . ."

"I, Mary, take thee, John, to be my wedded
husband . . ."

I include all those statements about loving and cherishing
"till death do us part."

I'm not using that sacred text as romantic nonsense! The
point that I underscore in reading it—and I make sure my
audience understands this—is that pledges between people
matter. I challenge my listeners to recollect the promises
they've made—to a spouse, to an employer, to a customer,
to a friend. Were they empty words, or have they been fulfilled? I bear down especially on the marriage pledge itself,
since I'm convinced that anything we say that deliberately
calls God to be the witness, as those vows do, better be able
to stand close examination.

Sometimes I've seen people blush or squirm when I do
this. I figure that's their problem, not mine. I'm not giving
my speech just to entertain them but to motivate them. And
my basic philosophy is that there's no motivation like Attitude, right thinking about people, which in turn always

leads to right behavior toward people. If it's still true, and I hope it is, that people's words should be as good as their bonds, I like to find out what giving their word means to them.

In the business realm it's extremely vital to have trust in each other. A man who is known to be cheating on his wife, to whom he has made one of life's most solemn, if not holy, commitments, can hardly be counted on with any certainty to keep the terms of a business deal. I had to associate with a number of such executives through the years who came to visit us or to do business with us at Holiday Inns, Inc., and who brought along their little black book so they could indulge in a fling while they were far away from home. It made me wonder.

An executive's attitude toward family, the priority placed on those intimate relationships with the nearest and dearest, is a sure clue to excellence.

I've commented earlier on the family sacrifices some people make in the interests of career advancement. In many cases, I've heard them justify what they do with the argument that it is ultimately for the family's sake. They want spouse and children to have the finer things in life, whatever those are. I find it hard to see family neglect as altruistic.

Is there anything finer, really, for growing boys and girls, than a parent's attention and affection, counsel and comradeship? What is a car or a horse or a boat or a trip compared to the warm security of belonging in someone else's heart? The so-called advantages that people think they are providing for their families through material goods are misleading if they are procured at the expense of close relationships.

The wholeness of an executive's life is not real if family life is broken or falling apart. The masquerade of success at the office wears very thin very soon when there is failure on the home front.

I've already alluded to my own family. Let me add that an executive who puts low priority on parental responsibilities is putting high obligations on the spouse. My wife, Geneva, was manager of the peewee baseball team that my two sons played on; she was den mother for the Cub Scout pack. She did the driving, almost all day long, from school to music lessons to sports events to dentist appointments. She supervised the housekeeping and saw that our four children—William and Rusty, Katherine and Geneen—were fed and clothed and bandaged for their bruises, both physical and emotional.

All of that was in addition to the responsibilities I expected her to fulfill as a corporate officer's wife—traveling with me to important events, attending company social functions, entertaining large groups of people in our home. There's no way to calculate the demands she had to face and bear with poise and grace. I don't know how Geneva stood up under it all; a lot of executive spouses can't.

I'm not describing an unusual situation, I know. The same is true to some degree, in varying detail, in every home where one parent is employed outside. I wonder, sometimes, what's happening these days in the vast number of homes where *both* parents are employed.

Based on my personal experience during those years when I tended to put work ahead of family and the lingering consequences of that neglect in their lives and my own, I can only hope that men and women who are so worldly-wise when it comes to corporate negotiations and business operations will have the sense and sensitivity to look to the welfare of their own flesh and blood offspring in those precious areas of the spirit that matter infinitely much.

The benefits of keeping family life in good repair, however, go beyond mere executive image and influence in some pragmatic ways that directly affect the conduct of business. People in management who are learning solid lessons at home about respecting personality differences, refereeing arguments, establishing a just system of disciplines and rewards, and offering motivational help can surely transfer much of that acquired wisdom to the relationships encountered daily in the workplace.

There are moments, for instance, when an associate may need a little spouselike comfort and advice, or when employees may need some parental firmness to counteract their childish flare-up on the job. Home is one of the best places in the world to observe and practice such basic human relations principles. I'm not saying that the boss has to be Big Daddy or Big Mama at the office; there are some other dynamics at work there. But insights gained from family relationships are widely applicable.

Here, too, you have a potential danger if you reverse the principle and try to run the household the way you run the office, with Mama or Daddy acting like boss. In the intimacy of the family circle, management techniques that work quite satisfactorily on the job require lots of flexibility and adaptation. Executives readily lose patience and get frustrated when orders aren't carried out at home with the same promptness and thoroughness expected at the office. The interests and schedules of children simply can't be regulated in identical ways to those used with employees. Parenting and presiding are two different ball games!

The fundamental to underscore, in the complexity of all this necessary give and take, is that God's gift of a spouse and children is unquestionably to be assigned higher priority than the job and civil responsibilities, the love of work and the love of country. Executives sadly delude themselves if they think that the family can wait until the job is done.

Families don't wait. They grow up and move on. If excellence is the goal—that Attitude which is the way—then it's the job that can wait, if need be, while the family is served.

Because of the concern for his family that prompted Kemmons to start his Holiday Inns in the first place, the company always in the early days catered to the special needs of parents and children, even though seventy percent of the business came from commercial travelers. Boys and girls under twelve could stay free of charge in their parents' room; baby beds were free; family pets not only were allowed, but were provided with kennels and food where local codes permitted; restaurant menus accommodated child-size appetites; and play equipment was available as well as the swimming pool.

We in the executive suite let it be known that we were family people, despite whatever shortcomings we might have had, and we expressed continual interest in the family welfare of our employees. In our house publication, *Holiday Inn Times,* we reported not only a corporate acquisition but a shipping clerk's appendectomy! We paid attention to what mattered to our workers, including their families, because we wanted them to know that we believed in and supported family values.

When there was illness or even death in employee ranks, the company was present through its chaplain and other staff people to give comfort and cheer. We weren't trying to be a substitute for a church but simply wanted to demonstrate that in our company, the Attitude of concern for the individual extended to spiritual ministry in time of crisis—a caring for the whole person. Since we said we were a family, we would act like family.

If the Attitude—right thinking about people—is the way to keep priorities straight, then family has to be right up there near the top, above country, above work. To downplay it invites disaster, both at home and in the office. Such an important sector of an executive's life cannot be a shambles without affecting adversely every other area.

But it's not until you get to life in the fourth dimension, to the top priority, that everything comes together in a coherent whole. The highest love that motivates our Attitude is really the foundational one, as well: the alpha and the omega.

Love for God.

Tune out when you read that, and you'll never understand the secret of the Holiday Inns miracle. Worse, you'll never approach excellence, no matter how hard you struggle to reach it.

According to a national survey, business executives are reluctant to admit, much less discuss, their private beliefs. They seem to think there's no connection between work and worship. I'm here to tell you that, for me, problems in the business community, in my family circle, and in my own soul would be both unbearable and unsolvable apart from spiritual benchmarks to guide me.

I know it's hard for a lot of business people, who are disciplined to think almost exclusively in terms of tangibles, to take God seriously. After all, God doesn't have an office where you make appointments to see him as you would your doctor or another executive. You can't present God with a form you've filled out showing all of your qualifications to be let into heaven when you die. Somehow, the whole matter seems so immaterial.

I never tried to make anyone believe I was a prophet. I just did what I thought was right, following my natural inclinations and trusting that to be God's way of answering my prayers, which were sincere. I was a conduit through whom God could work if he chose. I believe that he is due the credit for whatever we accomplished in the growing years at Holiday Inns.

Everybody who knows anything about the history of our company knows that we were a religious group. When *Institutions* magazine saluted Holiday Inns, Inc., with their annual Changemaker Award in 1973, editor Jane Young Wallace wrote:

> There was a time, in the early '60s, when it was considered "smart" to make fun of Holiday Inns. It wasn't hard. There was the less-than-pristine design of the Great Sign, the down-home drawls, the unfashionable and unashamed belief in God, America, and the success of Holiday Inns.

In the feature story of that October 15 issue, under the title "Are These People for Real?" the writer commented:

> Most of them are Southern. Many are deeply religious with a fundamentalist faith that pervades everything they do. They're deeply involved with people. They care.

Now, I'd say that was a very perceptive journalist! After all, we were a native institution in Memphis, Tennessee, which has sometimes been referred to as the Buckle on the Bible Belt. We do take our faith in God seriously in these parts.

What may have grown a bit dim in some memories, however, with all the controversy that developed over Holiday Inns getting into the operation of gambling casinos, is that the religious conviction referred to by so many writers and observers over the years was not the peculiar position of just one officer of the company, namely me!

Kemmons Wilson and I didn't see eye to eye on plenty of things, and we had our share of fights in the executive suite. But there was never any question about his reflecting admiration for his Methodist heritage.

And there surely was nothing vague about Wallace Johnson's solid Southern Baptist faith, and nothing veiled in his expression of it. Just after we got started, in the fourth issue of *Holiday Times* (March 1956), Wallace wrote,

> The rapid rise of a new star in celestial space—the star sign high above the Holiday Inns of America—can only be attributable to the grace and divine guidance of the Father of all things and the silent partner of all business successes . . .
>
> As president of Holiday Inns of America, Inc., I have asked God's divine guidance in the formation and promulgating of the policies and principles which form the basic foundation of the operation of Holiday Inns of America.
>
> I feel that Holiday Inns of America, Inc., has a heart and a soul, and as a human being must live by his principles, so must Holiday Inns of America, Inc., live by its principles.

He concluded that particular piece by a reference to the Golden Rule.

High-blown rhetoric? A lot of people think so. We were

scoffed at as country boys and religious nuts for saying things like that. But the sneers were premature.

Our religion wasn't some confused mixture of piety and patriotism. We were Christians in the biblical sense of believing something very specific about a particular historical person named Jesus Christ.

Again, Wallace, greeting employees through the *Times* at Christmas in 1971:

> The New Year will bring to you and your company, Holiday Inns, a new challenge around the world, and it is only with God's help that we can keep this great company moving around the great world of ours.
>
> . . . As we celebrate this Christmas season, let each of us keep in mind the birth of our Lord and Savior, Jesus Christ, and worship him in all that we do or say. And may God bless you today and many days on this earth.

The religious talk at Holiday Inns, Inc., was not some idiosyncrasy, or idiocy, of Bill Walton's. I was a lifelong Presbyterian, but I shared with Methodist Kemmons and Baptist Wallace a respect for basic New Testament Christianity that more than a billion people on this earth share this very day.

I hasten to say that I'm not a preacher, and much less am I a theologian. In my role as chief operating officer at Holiday Inns, Inc., for its first twenty years, I knew that I couldn't walk into a boardmeeting and start off by saying, "Now, brothers, I'm going to read you some Scripture and make a few edifying comments."

Not everyone in that boardroom, even from the very start, shared the spiritual beliefs of the cofounders. We had all stripes of persuasion among the franchisees, from Christians and Jews to agnostics. And there certainly was no religious test for people who wanted to join the working ranks of the Holiday Inns family.

It's a totally different matter, however, to argue that personal beliefs are to be kept in some kind of airtight compartment completely isolated from the daily affairs of business. The New Orleans *Times-Picayune* (November 19, 1969) quoted me as saying in a speech to the Kiwanis Club of that city:

"Religion and business can and must be compatible. The day and age of morality in business and in thinking is not gone."

Any other view is utter foolishness. It's like saying that breathing and walking are so different from each other that there can be no relationship between them. You just show me a walker who's stopped breathing, and I'll show you a zombie!

There are lots of zombies beautifully laid out in executive suites around the country. Wearing $700 suits, hair coiffed, nails manicured, surrounded by matched-grain walnut paneling and rent-a-plant greenery, they repose serenely in what's little more than a corporate coffin. The privileged admirers who are permitted access to this carpeted and draped hush come away commenting on how "natural" everything looks.

A zombie is still a zombie in any setting. Executives who have lost their breath (the Greek word, scholars tell me, is *pneuma*, meaning "wind" or "spirit") may keep up appearances and go through the motions for a while, but they are like dried cocoons after the moth has flown. Empty.

Spirit is that part of us human beings that is invisible, intangible, and indispensable to living. It's the number one priority in the very nature of things. Without it, we're dead.

Likewise, I as a human personality am not just an overweight lump of flesh cluttering the surface of the planet for a few decades and then dissolving into atoms. I am a consequence of many forces at work for generations before I appeared. And what I do while I'm here will produce consequences affecting populations yet to come.

There's something in me, as I understand it, that does matter, that makes a difference. It's my spirit. That's a mystery to me, but no less a reality. And it puts me into an Attitude of respecting the mystery of personality as a part of reality. It makes me willing to admit there are things to be known beyond what I know, and that there are unseen forces at work in the world beyond whatever influence I can exert.

At this point, I can react in one of two ways. I can slink in fear of the beyond. Or I can move forward with faith in the beyond. *Fear* and *faith* are small words, but they dominate our mental processes. Only one of them at a time, however, can control us, because they are mutually exclusive.

Fear is the father of a large family, including doubts, indecisions, alibis, and other negatives. As someone has well said, fear is the commander-in-chief over three very destructive generals: apathy, inertia, and procrastination. Obviously, the effect of fear is to immobilize us.

An immobilized executive is a contradiction in terms. By definition, an executive is one who carries out duties and functions, who administers affairs. For such a person paralysis would be fatal. People who cannot get things done never make it to the executive level. Nor can anyone stay at that level who loses drive and momentum.

Fear breeds failure.

Some executives, paralyzed by fear, fool their colleagues

and their constituents for a little while by a lot of noise that's mistaken for motion. Bluster and bluff are like deodorant, though: their effect wears off quickly, and then everything stinks!

When I was a boy, walking down the middle of a dark Memphis street at three in the morning on my way to pick up the newspapers for delivery on my route, I whistled and prayed to keep up my courage. I don't hesitate to admit I've done much the same thing since becoming a grown man, telling God my problems and worries. Fear stalks us all our life. There's always some new test coming along that makes our mouths dry and our palms wet with anxiety.

What's the secret of overcoming fear? I like the way the 1611 King James Version of the Bible puts it: "There is no fear in love; but perfect love casteth out fear" (1 John 4:18).

I can get a real clear mental picture of something being "cast out"—like Geneva and I have to do around the house every so often with some old item that's lost its usefulness and become junk.

But "perfect" love? That's an adjective I would have to be careful about applying to most anything. I surely wouldn't claim it for my own character or behavior. How, then, can that encourage me in my fight against fear?

By activating that other little word I mentioned: *faith*.

What that means hasn't always been clear to me, and I know just enough now to realize how little I know about it. But, in my own simple way as a layman, I can make this distinction at least: my boyhood whistling in the dark served mainly to shut out some of the scarier predawn sounds in the city. My more mature praying, by contrast, puts me in touch with a companion who is bigger and stronger and wiser than I. That gives me comfort and confidence.

Faith is our link to the Lord. I'm talking about much

more than an intellectual nod to an abstract theory that there must be a God of some kind somewhere. I mean by faith taking in trust the revealed Word, the Bible, which tells us what we need to know about God.

That trust, in turn, mysteriously and marvelously supplies me with strength to tackle difficult tasks and see them through to a successful conclusion.

A spiritual giant like Billy Graham, whom I admire so much, makes it a practice to read five Psalms and a chapter from the book of Proverbs in the Bible every day. If he finds that instructive for getting along with God and his neighbor, I can't afford to ignore it.

According to the Bible, then, which I take as my authority in matters of the spirit, the message that goes all the way back to the beginning of the human experience on earth is this:

God loves us.

God has a plan for us.

God fixed the link with himself that we broke by ignoring his law.

God takes us back into his fellowship without holding anything against us.

God invites us to join up with him in setting this whole world back on the right track.

God intends for us to keep on enjoying his company even after this life on earth is over.

Can you see what that message of his love can do for my fear? I am told that I am loved, that my life has purpose, that my mistakes are forgiven, that this world can be changed, and that the best is yet to come.

Believe me, that casts out my fear! I don't find that kind of message coming from any other source that I can have confidence in. The perfect love, it turns out, is God's love for me—not mine for him. He's way ahead of me, and the love I have for him is not my overture, but my response.

When I make up my mind to accept that ultimate truth, then faith has taken over. And when faith takes over, my spirit comes alive. Why? Because, through faith, I am restored to fellowship with the source of my being, I am hooked up to the power, and I am freed to function as I was designed.

If you are an executive zombie, the people who work with you in your organization or company are not going to be inspired ("spirited") by your example. That's why loving God as your top priority makes absolutely the best business sense imaginable.

Nothing in the science of motivational skills can possibly surpass the influence of a fearless and faith-filled leader! Knowing that, you can become the excellent executive you're meant to be . . . IF.

There's a question mark. How can an executive's personal love for God be translated into professional Attitude in business without seeming to impose it on others? You can't turn your routine business activities into some kind of old-fashioned camp meeting with hymn singing and preaching! At least, not if you don't own your own business where you can call all the shots.

Some folks will tell you that's exactly what we tried to do at Holiday Inns, Inc. Some of the directors used to say it in board meetings, for that matter. Well, let me review a couple of items to clarify. Then you can make up your own mind.

One cold, rainy day in 1956, I arrived on the executive scene. Kemmons and Wallace, nearly $40,000 in debt for the new motel business, needed some legal help to incorporate and deliver on their franchise promises, so I said "Sure" and shook hands.

They gave me office space in an old plumbing shop, where a cast-off plywood door laid across two packing cartons was my desk. My cherished dream of becoming a corporate executive had come true at last—but hardly as I'd imagined. I had always wanted to be, and do, and have the best. As a child, when I built clubhouses for the kids in the neighborhood, they were always super models, with trap doors and sliding windows and secret entrances. Now I was third in command in the new enterprise, the midwife who would bring it to birth.

But—in a plumbing shop?

I went into the back storage room and knelt down in the middle of the dirt floor. I must have stayed there an hour or more, asking God for help. I didn't have the specialized education or the business background to fully grasp then what was required of me. Would he, please, give me wisdom?

I didn't pray doubting that he *could*, but I really had to scrape for enough trust to believe that he *would*. I figured it was probably a good idea to make some promises, too, so I told him whatever resulted I'd try to use for the glorification of his kingdom.

It wasn't fancy, but it was honest.

In the sixteen years that followed, as we grew swiftly to become the largest company in our industry, the ingredients of that first simple prayer characterized all my petitions to God: dependence on his help and devotion to his honor. I've concluded that's the whole sum and substance of the matter, although experts in religion have tried to complicate it for me at times. If we honestly admit our need of God and aim to please him by what we do, life will stay in pretty good balance.

Executives who can't or won't admit their need for wisdom and strength from a source outside themselves, from God, really are putting themselves in the place of God. That's outright idolatry. When that attitude surfaces, employees catch on fast that stroking the boss's vanity is the highest good if you want to get ahead in that company. You can never again trust anything they say to your face.

This pandering to the uncontrolled personal egos of senior corporate officers is probably the most dangerous single condition in American business today. I was vulnerable to it all the time. At Holiday Inns, staff members and directors would constantly remind me what Bill Marriott was doing, or what Barron Hilton was doing, insinuating that surely Holiday Inns could outdo them. As a result, some of the actions we took slipped over that fine line between legitimate competitive edge and unbecoming ego satisfaction. It sounds real nice to be called "the greatest," even if you're the one saying it!

Security analysts from the stock exchange and the big brokerage houses bring unbelievable pressure to bear on corporations in this regard. They cater to ego trips by making executives of major corporations unduly conscious of their times-earnings ratio and their earnings per share, at the expense of proper attention to their percentage of reserves against accounts receivable. Common sense gives way to image building. Usually a deceived or defrauded public has to end up paying the piper.

Executives who pray with sincere humility for divine guidance and help will convey to their workers that people at the top don't have all the answers. That, in turn, rather than destroying employee confidence, encourages the rank and file to share their own insights on company problems and needs, thereby giving them a sense of participation that is strongly motivating to their best efforts.

With that rationale, convinced that senior management should set the example, I used my prerogatives—first as executive vice-president and then as president—to convene regular Wednesday morning executive prayer breakfasts at our headquarters in Holiday City.

That was a meeting in which we'd eat and then discuss the condition of the company, its plans, its forecasts. Someone in the group would lead in a prayer or maybe a Scripture reading. Then we'd have a brief program, usually a business or civic leader presenting a talk. It was primarily a time of informal fellowship.

At each annual meeting of our franchisees, the International Association of Holiday Inns (IAHI), I also scheduled a prayer breakfast on one of the mornings. This event usually drew an overflow crowd of 2,000 or more. Several times Dr. Billy Graham was our speaker.

Don't misunderstand this. We weren't trying to convert anybody. The Holiday Inn family members were respected for their individual convictions. Our purpose was not to proselytize but rather to underscore the fact that we who led the corporation sensed *our* need to draw upon higher resources than our own.

It was partly for the same reason that we added a chaplain to our corporate staff, knowing that many of our workers faced situations, both on the job and in their private lives, that called for counsel. Again, it was no intent to pressure people about religion, but just a company provision for one aspect of their lives where some extra help might be appreciated.

The same principles carried over into policies affecting

our guests. I issued a directive that the familiar Gideon Bibles, so generously provided by that fine organization for each guest room in hotel chains all over the world, should be taken out of the dresser drawer, where they were usually hidden, and placed on the table top, open. Each housekeeper's routine room inspection included checking on that Bible.

We organized a Chaplain-on-Call program that I mentioned earlier under the direction of the corporate chaplain, the Reverend Dub Nance. At one point, as many as 2,000 volunteer clergymen around the country were registered to counsel Holiday Inn guests who were suffering emotional or spiritual distress. We received many letters from travelers who valued this timely help when they were away from home. By some estimates, as many as 3,000 people may have been diverted from suicide attempts through a minister's guidance over the phone or at the inn. Between 1969 and 1976, while the program was in force, more than 250 news and feature articles about the program were published locally and nationally.

In addition, at several inn locations, we erected small meditation chapels on the grounds so that any guest who desired it could withdraw to a quiet haven to pray and contemplate. The first of these at a franchise location was dedicated at Don Weimer's inn in Forsyth, Georgia, in September 1972.

While some of the things we did were different from the usual, the spiritual concern was not unique. Industrial chaplaincies are quite widespread. I know there are a lot of individual executives even today who maintain an influential witness to their faith among their employees by quietly modeling a sincere commitment to God. Some of them place a Bible on their desks or spiritual mottoes on their walls. They bow their heads for prayer over meals in the company cafeteria or in the executive dining room. They talk freely about their church activities.

Wherever executives have the authority or privilege, however, they can do even more than that to create a corporate culture that reflects reverence for and reliance on God. It doesn't guarantee that every troublesome situation that comes up during a typical work day will be greeted with a "bless" instead of a "damn," but it helps.

The top priority: love for God.

Managerial excellence is a mockery if the factor of the spirit is missing. Like a wheel without a hub, there's nothing to hold the spokes together. Leadership style, management skills, personality strengths, and professional status—all of these are executive assets only if they reside in people who have got their priorities in order.

At the workplace, where they spend the better part of each week for most of their adult lives, people need examples of faith and fortitude. Management level people are the most conspicuous candidates to be that. If they approach the pile of daily problems with an upbeat attitude, they will instill the priceless quality of hope in the hearts of their people. And people with hope in their hearts are motivated to risk anything.

My files are bulging with letters from working members of the Holiday Inn family and from guests who stayed with us, testifying to the help they derived from the evidence of faith at work in the lives of corporate executives.

When Kemmons and Wallace gave me the initial challenge to set up the corporation with a constitution and bylaws so that we could go public, as well as to organize franchising for Holiday Inns into a system, I was almost naive enough to think that I could build a Christian company. I've learned long ago that there are no such things, because companies are mere legal entities.

Yet when executive priorities are in the right order, the truth of Shakespeare's words in *The Merchant of Venice* are confirmed:

"Earthly power doth then show likest God's."

Someone has made a plea for "creative business statesmanship" in our day, in contrast to "hyping the bottom-line performance." There can't be any impressive creativity when executives don't make room for the mysterious, for those possibilities that reach, as Thomas Huxley once said in a different context, "beyond the ken and scope of science."

What I believed then with all my heart, and still do to this day, is that you can build into the conditions in which people work a respect for the Judeo-Christian spirit of love for God that will result in wonders. That's why I wrote into the Holiday Inns purpose statement: " . . . that we intend to build a corporation and a business based on the recognition of the dignity of all people and on Christian principles, especially man's love for his fellow man."

God knows, we tried.

# Conclusion
## *The Bottom Line:*
# Integrity of the System

On the morning of March 16, 1974, a bomb burst in the Holiday Inns boardroom. Presiding at the directors' meeting, Kemmons Wilson called for items of new business.

J. B. Temple, head of Inn Operations and a member of the board for years, said he had a statement he wanted to enter in the record, since his full-time service with the company was scheduled to conclude in June. He began by paying a high tribute to the three of us—Kemmons, Wallace, and me. Then he offered eight recommendations "with sincerity and goodwill for the benefit of the company . . . "

He minced no words—and they are all a matter of open record, in accordance with the laws governing publicly held corporations. As he proceeded, one could detect the rising blood pressure rate in several of us around the table.

One of his recommendations criticized the various religious dimensions of our corporate life—prayer breakfasts and the chaplaincy in particular. He felt that they were being pushed on other executives who didn't necessarily hold similar beliefs and that they were inappropriate in a public company.

I knew J. B. to be a man of strong convictions. He was perfectly within his rights to make such a valedictory statement, and he was careful to do it in a good spirit of company concern. His own fourteen-year record of service to the corporation was an example to everybody of the kind of enlightened leadership that paid off handsomely in the growth of his division to front rank.

I'm sure that every one of us in the room went along with him on several of his recommendations. In fact, he had the courage to voice things that had been seething below the surface for months or longer and that no one else up to that point had dared to bring into the open.

You can guess, however, that I was boiling inside over that religion issue.

In the first place, no one was ever brought onto the executive staff at Holiday Inns without knowing where we in top management were coming from. They didn't have to agree with us in matters of faith and practice, but the media as well as the company records had fully exposed our convictions from day one.

Typical headlines might read: "Walk with God, Executive Urges" (Wichita); "God and Mammon at Holiday Inns" (San Francisco); or this winner from *Wall Street Journal*: "Room Service? Send 3 Bourbon, 2 Scotch—And One Chaplain"!

On that March morning in 1974, we three cofounders were occupying the three top positions in the company, with a twenty-year history of making our viewpoint clear. Anybody who joined us knew what they were getting into philosophically. It was that same familiar Holiday Inns motif of "no surprises."

I know that J. B. was not denying our privilege to believe whatever we wanted to. His argument was that we were pushing our creed and code on the rest of them.

I'd like to deny that charge outright.

But I'm not sure that I can.

It was never my intention to force others to accommodate to my set of beliefs about God, but you can tell from things I've said that my personal and professional attitudes were very largely a seamless fabric. Where one stopped and the other began would be hard to discover. I have to admit, therefore, that I probably laid on others, unconsciously much of the time, expectations that they resented.

In my files I have come across at least one note that I sent to three key executives following one of our prayer breakfasts where they were conspicuous by their absence. It was a rebuke for their nonattendance, and it did come from the president's office. There is pressure in that as well as intimidation. My aim was well-meaning, but my handling of the matter probably left something to be desired.

What I'm getting at is this: in our human fallibility, we will inevitably botch up now and again, failing to be as sensitive as we should be to others and failing to be as skillful as the situation requires. We need to be sorry when that happens and not get on the defensive.

Whenever an executive begins a statement with the words "Because of my position," watch out! What comes next will likely appeal to executive authority, privilege, or status. It's shifty ground.

On the other hand, every person in management should operate by the priorities that spring from deeply held convictions so that living and making a living aren't boxed off from each other.

Part of managerial skill, of course, includes the capacity to compromise when there are differing opinions about a course of action. Problems are bound to follow, though, when the compromise involves one's individual convictions. To go against conscience is demoralizing ("de-moral") and sets the fuse on a self-destruct mechanism. Sooner or later a demoralized person will blow up and go to pieces. The fallout showers trouble on the whole company.

There's a single word to cover the idea of holding together instead of falling apart, and I used it constantly at Holiday Inns as the other side of the Attitude coin.

The word is *integrity*.

Few people understand its meaning. In popular usage it seems to be interchangeable with *honesty*. We say, "She's a woman of integrity. You can trust her word." Or, "He's a man of integrity. He always makes a fair deal."

That's great as far as it goes, but integrity means a whole lot more than that. There's no excellence without it, that's certain, so it better be understood in its fullest sense.

When we talk about integrating, we mean combining separate elements into a common entity without destroying the individual characteristics.

When we describe something as integral, we mean that it is a part inseparable from other parts but not indistinguishable from them. Both nature and function are involved in the process. Individuality is preserved and honored at the same time that harmony is generated.

Integrity, then, means "wholeness," in contrast to fragmentation or incompleteness. It describes "getting it all together," in contrast to "coming apart"—which we call *dis*integration.

"Integrity of the System," as I said, played counterpoint to "Attitude toward People" in my conception of management at Holiday Inns, Inc. Considering the tremendous diversity of men and women affiliated with us in the parent company and in the franchise network, along with their private persuasions and preferences, we could have ended up as just one gigantic kaleidoscope, with relationships changing unpredictably at every adjustment the management team made. It would have been colorful—and chaotic!

The first time I talked to the franchisees back in 1956, I knew that the biggest challenge was to get them working together, since they were all entrepreneurs who were accustomed to going it alone. That's when the system was born.

It was not to be a motley collection of free agents doing their own thing under our name. In American business up until then, that kind of loose coalition had worked reasonably well in things like automobile dealerships and chain stores, because the product quality and performance were predetermined by the manufacturers.

In our case, as a service industry, we had to find ways to standardize performance so that the public would know what it could count on when it stopped at a Holiday Inn. As we planned our services and presented them to the franchisees, the issue of consistency was uppermost in our thinking. We made no apologies for insisting that things be done in the same way at every inn location.

In later years, a rebel would turn up now and then who wanted to violate some agreed-upon franchise standard. Then we had to bear down all over again on the principle of integrity of the system.

By and large, the owners bought into the concept gladly from the very start, partly because we were careful to give them a voice—and a vote—in designing those standards they would be compelled to observe. When I asked their opinion, they knew I wasn't just going through the motions. They were just as indignant as the parent company when renegades would try to break the pattern, and they read them out of the system without hesitation.

One of the slogans we found useful in communicating the system idea, as well as in coordinating staff efforts in the company, was "52 to the Right," football terminology for a signal called. Drawing the analogy of teamwork, I pointed out that no game can ever be realistically undertaken unless every signal will be followed by every member of the team.

"Fifty-two to the Right" meant realistic discussion of opportunities "in the huddle," and evaluations within our respective spheres of knowledge. But it also meant that once a decision was made, once the signal was called, every player had to perform cooperatively what he or she did best in order to achieve the goal.

Such performance is a blend of the finest talents of a group of individuals who will run just a little harder, stretch just a little farther, think just a little longer to make a project successful. In giving of themselves that way, they would ultimately realize their own strengths.

The impact of this uniformity reached to the remotest employee, of course, not just to the owners and innkeepers. A breakdown could occur at any one of a thousand points in daily operations at a local inn, not just in policymaking at the executive level. For that reason, we never let up on our insistence that workers' training include philosophy as well as policy and practice. They needed to understand why it was so vital to the company that they go by the book in their routine duties.

For the system to have integrity, all of our fascinating diversity had to be coordinated without being obliterated and regulated without being suffocated. The franchise contract, the operating manual, the training programs at the university and in the field, the annual conferences, and the never-ending stream of communications from headquarters throughout the worldwide system were means to that end.

It baffles me how major corporations can get themselves into such managerial tangles when the principle of integrity is waiting in the wings just begging to be brought on stage. The three-ring circus is tame in comparison to the diffusion of seemingly unrelated activities going on all at the same time in many companies. It's no wonder that top executives lose control and come down with ulcers or coronaries.

To say that, however, brings me back to the focus of this whole discussion: managerial excellence. It's futile to talk about the need and the means for producing integrity of the business system if the one in the driver's seat fails to get it all together personally.

Executives tend to be single-minded. Ordinarily that's considered a virtue, especially when there's an important job to get done and somebody has to give it undivided attention. Focus and concentration are good.

It's also a virtue to be single-minded about purpose. Every company needs a clearly defined driving force that motivates its planning and production. The people in top management are responsible to identify this and to see that the application of it is unswerving.

But it's so easy for the single-minded executive to become narrow-minded without detecting the difference. When you focus, you also eliminate. The term *tunnel vision* suggests the problem: inability to perceive the big picture, the whole scene. Under those circumstances, it's more likely that the leader will have a blind side, too, taken by surprise by something that could and should have been expected but was not because attention was fixed too narrowly.

Executives must have not only the long view but the broad view. They need to keep track of each and every part, while at the same time they see how the parts fit together to make up the whole. They have to constantly make value judgments on the respective merits of proposals in the light of their expanded perspective. To the specialists who work for them, they have to be interpreters of seemingly unrelated moves that have to be orchestrated carefully to produce the desired effect.

If executives let themselves become preoccupied with pet projects of their own inside or outside of company concerns, or if they let themselves be conned by fast-talking enthusiasts into approving minor things to receive major effort, business will head for breakdowns. The person at the top absolutely *must* see the enterprise steadily and see it WHOLE.

At Holiday Inns, it was ticklish enough that I had to cope with an adventuresome entrepreneur like Kemmons who was forever coming up with new schemes for diversifying our activities, but I also was surrounded by bright young executives who each thought that their particular departments should be the tail that wagged the dog. You don't want to stifle initiative by being hostile to fresh ideas, but you sure can't be a pushover for every safari into new territory if you're going to run a responsible operation.

The inevitable question, of course, is how to cultivate this wholeness of vision, this integrity that constitutes executive excellence. In my opinion, after all I've seen and experienced, it's a question that's far more personal than professional. You have to be a certain kind of individual.

Basically, you have to be a person of integrity yourself. Diplomas and trophies have nothing to do with it. Titles have nothing to do with it. Membership in church or lodge or service club has nothing to do with it.

As you look around your office, how many symbols of

tribute to your leadership hang on the walls or line the shelves or accent your desk? Or does modesty forbid your displaying them? Is it upsetting to be told that none of those can be offered as evidence of your personal integrity?

We talk a lot about the bottom line in the business and financial communities. For us it means primarily the dollar figure of profit or loss. But society has taken it over as a metaphor equivalent to "It all comes down to this," or, "In the final analysis," or, "When everything's said and done."

What's the bottom line on your personal integrity?

I ask myself that question right now. Do I have it all together, or have I gone to pieces? How can I tell? What can I do about it?

I wish I could present myself as Exhibit A of an integrated individual. It would be so simple if I could just say: "Look at me. Take your cues from my life."

But I can't say that, regrettably. In honest self-examination, I discover lots of fragmentation in me. I'm not complete, in the sense that I do everything I should and that I feel the right way about everything. I'm still learning and still trying.

It's immensely encouraging to come across a statement like this in the New Testament: "But we have this treasure in earthen vessels, that the excellency of the power may be of God, and not of us" (2 Corinthians 4:7).

As I listen for the Lord's voice—through reading the Bible, through participating in church life, through counseling with spiritually mature friends—some things are slowly changing. My bitterness has been dissolving a little at a time. My purpose for moving on into the future has been getting clearer. There are places in my heart where peace has edged out conflict. But I've by no means arrived, even now that I've reached the age of retirement.

If you see much the same picture when you look at yourself, whatever your present age, maybe you get discouraged like I do sometimes. But I do believe I can offer you some cheer that will help you keep going.

Let me boil it down to its essence.

First, integrity, or a life in balance, or personal wholeness has had one perfect model in the person of Jesus Christ. I can know what the ideal is by looking at him—his words, his deeds. I don't have to stumble around in the fog trying to figure out what I'm looking for. He's it. The example.

Second, integrity in my own life, since I am not Jesus Christ, is not going to come by any amount of my struggling to achieve it through following his example. The good news is that God's mercy plants integrity in me if I'm willing, and his grace grows it in me while I'm in the very middle of tests and challenges. In other words, Jesus Christ is more than the perfect example of integrity. He is the provider of it, if we're open.

In that first instance, Jesus certainly modeled the Attitude I have been discussing. One of his clearest demonstrations of it may come as a shock to those who ignorantly stereotype him as a kind of namby-pamby do-gooder.

In the harshest language he ever used, he denounced the hypocrisy of his hearers, exposing their lack of integrity. Who were they? Harlots and thieves? No. They were *executives*, believe it or not, the ones often referred to in the biblical accounts as the rulers of the Jewish people—lawyers, teachers, and priests who jointly ran the system.

And what an elaborate system it was. Not anything as simple and straightforward as the Ten Commandments, but hundreds of regulations that determined daily life. And not just public observances, such as worship at the temple, but household routines like dishwashing!

Jesus had no use for such legalistic nit-picking when it

obscured what he called "the weightier matters of the law." On the occasion recorded in the Gospel of Matthew, chapter 23, this courageous carpenter picked up the hammer of God's truth and smashed the pious facade of the leaders to splinters.

I'm not going to give you an exhaustive verse-by-verse Bible lesson now. But an examination of the incident brings to light seven elements in personal integrity without which no leader in any field can perform with excellence. As you look at this list, maybe you'll understand better why I have insisted that Attitude is all.

According to Jesus, a leader who has integrity demonstrates that wholeness of character by:

1. Consistency between words and deeds (verse 3).
2. Acceptance of personal responsibility (verse 4).
3. Willingness to serve in humble ways (verses 6, 11, 12).
4. Deference to new people coming on the scene (verse 13).
5. Discernment between actuality and appearance (verse 16).
6. Understanding of priorities (verse 23).
7. Harmony between morality (beliefs) and ethics (behavior) (verses 25, 28).

That's a pretty comprehensive outline of what it takes to be a master in human relations, which is what every manager worthy of the name is expected to be.

There's no excuse in saying, "You can't expect me to be perfect." As a matter of fact, in his famous Sermon on the Mount, which many people accept as a part of their philosophy of life regardless of their theological convictions, Jesus said, "Be perfect, as God is perfect."

What are we going to do with that? Simply dismiss it as impossible, an exaggeration, a poor choice of words by Jesus?

If we dismiss it, with whatever rationalization, we eliminate the highest motivational incentive known to humanity—that there's an ideal to be sought. Nevertheless, its achievement lies beyond the best of us.

Where does that leave us? With a need for help. And who can give it, if nobody's perfect? The only one is God, who has commanded it.

And he does help. With his commissioning comes his equipping. He never requires from us something we don't have unless he supplies it for us.

Human integrity, then, of a quality that pleases God, comes from God as a gift, which we have the opportunity and responsibility to use on an everyday basis in working through the situations that challenge us.

I'm not talking religion. I'm talking relationship. I'm talking about a pilgrimage through this life in the company of a guide who has experienced everything we'll ever face and knows the way home. I'm talking about being humble enough to accept the provision God makes through Jesus Christ to turn a sinner like me into an acceptable son.

Jesus said to his questioning followers, "I am the way. Both the truth and the life." Both principle and practice.

He didn't say, "I *show* the way . . . I *teach* the truth . . . I *model* the life."

He said: "I AM."

To put it as plainly as I know how, then: integrity is a case of depending on God instead of on myself.

Maybe that was easier for me to take seriously than for some other people at Holiday Inns, Inc. I realized that with my limited education I didn't have the specific technical know-how to fill such a responsible position. I was positive that I had to have God's help, a solid rock to stand on, or I'd go under.

Although I failed to follow through with that wisdom more times than I want to think about, I aimed to be a good man as well as a good manager. That's why I insisted on keeping up our standards and why I tried to incorporate into them not only the letter of the law, but the spirit as well.

I thought it was beneficial to our people to reiterate the Christian principle of love for neighbor on which our business ideal was founded and to support it with practical aids for the spiritual side of their lives.

To my way of thinking, there was nothing incongruous with our business commitment to say "Love your neighbor" and to say "Pray for your neighbor" at the same time.

As I saw it, there was no inconsistency between our saying to our guests at the inns, "We care about you and want you to be comfortable," and saying to them, "There's a chaplain on call if you need comfort and want to talk to someone."

How can we truly express our caring for people if we give them only soap and soup without any sympathy for their hurts?

Where is our integrity, our wholeness, if we offer rest for the body but none for the soul?

Other companies, other businesses, will have to try to find their own means of fulfilling their own mandates to the people they are meant to serve. At Holiday Inns, Inc., we set our course in the beginning as we perceived it to be compatible with our commitment.

It's never easy.

But excellence wouldn't be excellence if it were commonplace. The word has become almost a cliché by now, which is too bad. Its meaning, however, is unimpaired by the overexposure.

And the need for it to be demonstrated everywhere, not only in the executive suite, was never more crucial than now.

In all of the current management craze about excellence, as if it were a new discovery, it's both humbling and instructive to be reminded that the secret has been an open one for several thousands of years in Jewish and Christian history.

Back in the days of Moses, some 1,500 years before Christ, that great lawgiver put it this way:

"Thou shalt love the Lord thy God with all thy heart, and with all thy soul, and with all thy might" (Deuteronomy 6:5).

When Jesus was asked what the greatest commandment was, he quoted those very words.

It's plain enough, isn't it? If you're going to get it all together—heart, soul, strength—there has to be a central unifying factor. The Bible says it's love for God.

In Jesus' response to his questioner, he didn't stop with quoting the words of Moses from Deuteronomy but added, as the commandment just like it, what Moses wrote in Leviticus (19:18):

"Thou shalt not avenge nor bear any grudge against the children of thy people, but thou shalt love thy neighbor as thyself."

That completes the secret. Get the vertical relationship with God in proper alignment, and it follows that the horizontal relationship with neighbor will fall into place.

The Apostle John said you can't have the one without the other:

"If a man says, 'I love God,' while hating his brother,

he is a liar. If he does not love the brother whom he has seen, it cannot be that he loves God whom he has not seen" (1 John 4:19, 20).

Talk about integration! Talk about integrity!

"Well and good," someone might say, "but I'm not the religious type."

What's that supposed to mean? That good human relations don't count? Even the atheistic humanist doesn't say that.

"But what's the big idea of mixing all this love talk with a discussion of excellent business management? Efficient executives are efficient whether they like people or not."

Agreed. But you can't simply use the words *excellent* and *efficient* interchangeably. Machines are efficient, but they don't have an Attitude. Slavedrivers have a horrible attitude toward humanity, but they're efficient. Is that excellence? Only a sadist would sanction that.

Executives are gifted with many skills that make them effective in their management of workers, or they wouldn't have gotten into positions of high reponsibility. They are usually pretty good judges of character, pretty good analyzers of problems, pretty good organizers of effort. But "pretty good" isn't "excellent" in any standard vocabulary.

The Apostle Paul, another leader with tremendous integrity, had a God-given insight on this that has become a classic by any reckoning. In a letter of his to some people in the city of Corinth, Greece, about 2,000 years ago, this brilliant scholar outlined a whole list of skills that are parceled out to different individuals by God. When he finished discussing their tremendous value to a community of faith, he urged his readers to covet the very best of them.

But then he shifted his direction abruptly by saying, "Let me show you a more excellent way."

More excellent than what? Than sheer possession of skills or use of talents. And, note this, a "way," an attitude, not an ability.

What was the "more excellent way" he had in mind?

The thirteenth chapter of First Corinthians spells it out: love. If you haven't got that, Paul said, you haven't got anything. If you haven't got that, nothing you do with your gifts and abilities counts for anything.

*Love is the way of excellence.* Love for God. Love for neighbor.

Integrity—wholeness—exists only where the vertical and horizontal dimensions are precisely aligned. Then everything comes together. Then everything works together.

And when everything comes together and works together in your personal life and in your business career, you will be recognized not only as an excellent executive, but better still, as an excellent *person.*

That kind of person is a leader. The most influential motivational force is personal example.

Speaking in the advanced chaplain course at the Air Force University at Maxwell Air Force Base in Alabama in March, 1983, I commented, "Motivation by example is directly related to, and supported by, true sincerity. Nothing is so apparent as hypocrisy—on the part of an individual, an organization, or a nation."

The thing that other business leaders always had such a hard time figuring out about us officers at Holiday Inns was how we could get away with some of the policies and practices I've described. I hope I've made the answer clear.

Attitude. Integrity.

If all that I've said is true, why wasn't Holiday Inns, Inc., included in the primary list of excellent companies reported on by Peters and Waterman? I can't be sure of the reason, or reasons, of course. But I do remember Dr. Peters saying in a television interview that one key item in their selection criteria was that any company under consideration still be operating according to its founding principles.

To put it bluntly: Holiday Inns did not so operate.

The newly appointed president of the company, Mike Rose, was quoted in the *New York Times* on August 5, 1979, as saying:

> The company outgrew a lot of people and their talents . . . The tougher business environment of the 70s went beyond their capabilities and others didn't like the new pace . . . There's no one from the old group left . . . Free-standing restaurants and casino hotels are a logical extension of the hospitality business and have a synergy with them. Roy and I have been the prime movers in these areas. Prior management couldn't bring themselves to making these decisions.

In a story in *Barrons,* under the by-line of James Grant and datelined Memphis, the statement was made: "For most of the past three years, Holiday has cultivated its garden. It has pruned its run-down properties and, by its own account, rid top management of 'bums.' "

In his "Money Tree" column in the *San Francisco Chronicle* on September 8, 1979, under the headline "God and Mammon at Holiday Inns," Milt Moskowitz wrote in part:

> Holiday Inns, the greatest lodging chain ever built, is turning its back on some principles held dearly by its founders—and everyone is applauding. . . .
>
> There was an evangelical feeling to Holiday Inns in its early days, a feeling that came out of the Southern Chris-

tian background of its leaders . . . William B. Walton . . . once told a reporter:

"At our first board meeting we were determined to build a company based on recognition of the dignity of man and on Christian principles of the brotherhood of man."

Last month it was all coming together for Holiday Inns. The company acquired a 40-percent interest in the Riverboat casino on the Las Vegas Strip. A few days later it sold its Trailways subsidiary for $100 million, which will be used to enter the Atlantic City gambling scene in concert with Harrah's.

So Holiday Inns is out of buses and into slot machines. . . .

Now you know why, in 1979, I took a leave of absence to my retirement—which became effective early in 1985. At the time, I wore the title Vice-Chairman of the Board Emeritus, and I was the only one of the three cofounders still on the company roster.

What had happened?

To use an Old Testament parallel, a Pharaoh arose who knew not Joseph. Kemmons Wilson retired in July 1979, and Roy Winegardner became chairman and chief executive officer, with Mike Rose as president.

About five years before that, the fiscal crisis that developed through unwise acquisitions and the oil embargo combined to send the company stock plunging from its high above 55 to an abysmal 4+. Boardroom panic spurred the directors to consider the company's entry into operation of gambling casinos.

The debate about it actually went on for several years. To consider such action, under our constitution and by-laws, it was necessary to amend the rules of operation, which expressly forbid any such activity on Holiday Inns premises.

The original regulation banned pinball machines, juke-boxes, or other "coin-operated gambling, amusement, or music device," as well as "obscene literature." (People had kidded me for years that we tolerated at least one slot machine in our Holiday Inn lobbies: the postage stamp dispenser!)

The board couldn't act without careful deliberation. But I couldn't buy the proposed solution.

Roy, who had joined the board in 1974 as senior vice-chairman, second in command to Kemmons, came over to my house, just across the road from his in suburban Memphis, to urge me to stay out of the whole affair. I believe he sincerely wanted to spare me hurt. He and I had been friends from the very beginning, when he became one of our first and largest franchise holders. We had sat in board meetings together sharing dismay that mergers and diversified conglomerations were draining the company's capital resources. He approached the chairmanship determined to "get rid of the whiskers," as he put it, and to bring the company back on track.

To do that, Roy and my immediate successor as president, L. M. Clymer, perceived the burgeoning casino empires in Nevada and in New Jersey, as "good for business." Roy was furious, as anybody would be, that his heavy stock holdings had suffered such drastic paper losses, and he wanted to recoup. I certainly couldn't blame him for that, because my far more modest holdings were just as badly affected.

At last, in December 1975, the president of the company made the motion that we enter the gaming business in Las

Vegas. That motion failed, eight to seven. When it was brought up again, in September 1977, the motion passed with only three opposed. A year later, when it was moved to permit gambling operations in any company location where it was legal, and specifically in Atlantic City, I was the only member of the board still recorded as voting against the proposals. I was told in no uncertain terms that there was no longer any place in the company for my kind of thinking.

(Incidentally, along with such action there was also approval of a change in our rules of operation that permitted "offensive" magazines to be displayed on the counter or rack as long as there were certain viewing restrictions.)

For me, those developments presented an intolerable situation. I see gambling as a destructive force that lures easily duped people to spend money they can ill afford in a futile attempt to get instant wealth—at the risk of their own livelihood. That struck me as being the very antithesis of everything we had promoted through the Holiday Inns Attitude for two dozen years.

Respect . . . Love.

How does bleeding the public at the gaming tables, knowing many will be hurt or even ruined financially, jibe with that? Was this a demonstration of what "service industry" meant? A service it was, indeed—to greed and gullibility.

Well, the corporation's bottom line shows that the new ventures did, in fact, turn out to be good for business. The stock, according to the 1983 annual report, reached an all-time high at midyear. The revenue dollars have rolled in to the newly renamed Holiday Corporation by the tens of millions, out of the pockets and purses of high-rollers and grinders (average wage earners) alike.

My question is: do the corporate winnings justify the public losses?

Or is it all a commentary on our times? Are the people conditioned by materialistic appeals on every hand to get all they can instead of give all they can? The fact that gambling is legalized in many places, and that state-operated lotteries are creating instant millionaires, does not change its essential nature.

Writing in the *New York Times* (August 25, 1985), columnist William Safire gets right to the point:

> State governments have found a way to soak the poor, and the poor are lapping it up: Ten billion dollars a year is now being extracted legally from the pockets of the suckers . . . Today 21 state governments not only participate in, but actively promote, what used to be considered a reprehensible activity: exploiting the desire to get rich quick without work. Off-track betting parlors operated by the state compete with the latest state-sponsored lottery vending machines for a piece of the poor man's payroll, and clergymen complain only because it is cutting into bingo profits.

Mr. Safire's words: "exploiting" . . . "suckers." I rest my case.

My nostalgia for the Holiday Inns miracle is partly for the trappings, I suppose—the gaudy Great Sign with its flashing star, the Gideon Bible on the bedside table, the grand openings of new inns. But I hope it goes deeper than that. I hope I miss it because it had about it the quality of caring, a desire to be of service that would help every traveler to believe in people as much as we did.

Yes, there is a more excellent way. It's costly. But it

produces true integrity, making lives whole instead of draining and fragmenting them.

A leader in business, therefore, who wants to substantiate any claim to being people-centered in company policy and practice, will wisely acknowledge that final accountability is to a higher authority than auditors or market analysts. Only then is integrity a personal reality.

The Attitude of love is the way to business excellence. And *that* is the bottom line.